The
C H R O N I C L E S
of
Dr. Sunday

QUOTE: MALALA YOUSAFZAI! "ONE TEACHER, ONE PEN,
ONE BOOK, CAN CHANGE THE WORLD" - ANSWERS TO:
'THAT'S WHAT I'M TALKIN' ABOUT!!!

authorHOUSE

AuthorHouse™
1663 Liberty Drive
Bloomington, IN 47403
www.authorhouse.com
Phone: 833-262-8899

Published by AuthorHouse 09/23/2020

ISBN: 978-1-6655-0000-5 (sc)
ISBN: 978-1-6655-0001-2 (e)

Library of Congress Control Number: 2020917617

Print information available on the last page.

Any people depicted in stock imagery provided by Getty Images are models,
and such images are being used for illustrative purposes only.
Certain stock imagery © Getty Images.

This book is printed on acid-free paper.

Because of the dynamic nature of the Internet, any web addresses or links contained in this book may have changed
since publication and may no longer be valid. The views expressed in this work are solely those of the author and do
not necessarily reflect the views of the publisher, and the publisher hereby disclaims any responsibility for them.

A WHOLE NEW WORLD.

General Information

Higher 'spirituality'
Speaking volumes

WHAT YOU'RE READING HERE IS THE YOURS TRULY;
MODERN DAY 'GOSPEL ACCORDING TO' RELIGION AND
POLITICS; 'REFORMATION' SWEEPING THE NATION...

((KEY NOTE: ABOUT THE AUTHOR AND BOOK:))

THE YOURS TRULY, 'SOUL SAVING' PRODIGIOUS DR. OF A SICK SOCIETY;

- WAS HOME SCHOOLED BY GOD, BY WAY IN BECOMIMG
'PROFOUNDLY THE DEVIL'S WORST NIGHTMARE...

= STORIES AS THEY WERE ONCE WRITTEN AT THAT POINT IN TIME. =

= P–A–N–D–E–M–I–C =

MASK'UM
IF YOU
GOT'UM!!!

THE 'CRY WOLF' CHRONICLES

WHAT IS COVID-19? ANSWERS TO: IT'S A MULTITUDINOUS GUN SALES PROMOTION!
WHAT IS COVID-19? - IT'S A PRO-BASE-BALL PITCHER WITH A COMMANDING CURVE BALL, THAT
EVERYONE IN THE 'MAJOR LEAGUES' IS TRYING TO FLATTEN! 'I KNOW I, ONLY WENT 1 FOR 4,
IN TOILET PAPER SHOPPING...

BOOK CONTENTS STORY-LINE, OR WHAT YOUR READING HERE IS THE GOSPEL
ACCORDING TO 'RELIGION AND POLITICS' REFORMATION CHALLENGE; (VS)
THE DISPIRITED STATUS QUO. "WE'RE ALL IN THIS TOGETHER"? YEAH RIGHT!
'TRUE OVERPOPULATION IS WHEN THE MASSES DON'T HAVE A SNOW BALLS CHANCE
IN HELL OF EVER OBTAINING A QUALITY OF LIFE EXISTANCE. 'TOSS IN THE
ECONOMIC SET BACKS FOR ALL THOSE LAID-OFF PAYCHECK TO PAYCHECK LESS-
FORTUNATE; AND IT'S DOWN RIGHT SCARY OUT THERE; PROFOUNDLY 'WAKE-UP
AND SMELL THE C-O-P-Y'. EVIL AWAKENING! 'THE CORONAVIRUS PANDEMIC' IS
A ACT OF GODZILLA; THUS WE'RE ALL AT WAR WITH THIS INVISIBLE ENEMY.
'IS CONSTIPATION THE NEW NORM? 'WELCOME TO THE TWILIGHT ZONE; WHEREAS
IN KEEPING ONE'S SOCIAL DISTANCE; WE'VE ALL BECOME 'SPACE CADETS' AND
PHONE SEX IS NO LONGER CONSIDERED AS BEING KINKY. CABIN FEVER HYSTERIA?
'EVER SINCE THE SPORTS WORLD DIED; I WAS HOPING THAT WE'D RUN ACROSS
SOME 'GOOD SPORTS' AND YET THERE'S ALL KINDS OF 'PLAYERS' OUT THERE
THAT ARE HORDING TOILET PAPER, AND HAND SANITIZER, AND THAN CLAIMING
THAT THEIR HANDS ARE ALL CLEAN! - ALONG WITH ALL THOSE CURE-ALL $SCAM
ARTIST OUT THERE THAT WANT TO TOUCH THE FACE OF YOUR POCKET BOOK; AND
LAST BUT NOT LEAST; THE AGITATED CONVENIENT STORE AND BANK
ROBBERS OUT THERE FROM NOT HAVING ANY ACCESS TO OBTAINING FACE
MASKS; LEADING US INTO THIS 'ALSO BEING A ECONOMIC PANDEMIC.

OLD-SCHOOL REVISITED WITH THE BACK TO SQ ONE; 'DRUGS NOT HUGS' SOCIETY !
'HELL! ——— THESE ARE JUST SOME OF THE 'PERCEPTIVE FACTS' OUT THERE.
- AS FOR ME; I'M JUST LONGING FOR THE DAY THAT I CAN WASH MY FACE AGAIN...

"LEADERSHIP" SHOWCASE

'ASIAN BACKLASH' BECAUSE OF THE VIRUS?!
(TO THE RESCUE)
'DON'T LET STUPIDITY REIGN...

'TAKE THE SOLID CITIZEN·CHALLENGE!

- BY WAY OF A YOURS TRULY, COIN PHRASING THIS HERE PRAYER LIKE
STATEMENT. - CAN 'YOU SAY THAT - "'YOU TRULY LOVE EVERY WELL BEHAVED
PERSON ON THE PLANET?" - THUS SUPPRESSING 'RACISM' VIA A CATCH PHRASE.

♪ WHO ARE YOU ? —▷

'1st PAGE KNOCK OUT!!!

HIS TIME IS now

Atrocities of Democracy. "where to begin"

2012 FAITH FORUM *Do all religions offer a path to God?*

THE GOOD NEWS MINE DOES 24/7 — 365.. THE BAD — DEMOCRACY DEPRIVED 'THIS ONE'S BEEN BIG TIME 'ROAD BLOCKED' FOR DECADES.'

'MAKE MY DAY'.

Imagemakers "stop this cover-up!"

"WHAT WE HAVE 'HERE' IS A FAILURE TO COMMUNICATE".

* "**The world according to** *The* MESSIAH?"

'YOURS TRULY, 'CLASSROOM SAVIOR OF THE WORLD'; IN A SOCIETAL 'HOW TO' NEUTRALIZE SANITY INTO' ILLICIT PEOPLE, BY WAY OF —

PROGRAMING PERSONAL "JUDGEMENT DAY" WAKE-UP CALL

'RESPONSIBILITY.

"R-E-A-D-I-N-G-B-E-T-W-E-E-N-T-H-E-L-I-N-E-S"

(((WELCOME TO " REVERSE PSYCHOLOGIES FINEST HOUR!")))

"ALL GOD'S CHILDREN, HISTORIC INAUGURAL DECLARATION".

"I AM YOU, AND YOU ARE ME; AND YOU ARE ME, AND I AM YOU".,

ALL ONE IN THE SAME PEOPLE, RESPONSIBLE FOR THE SAFETY AND

WELL BEING OF ALL PEOPLE. 'AS IN BEING RELATIVE TO FAIRNESS, 'ETC'

ALL BIRDS OF A FEATHER CREATED EMOTIONALLY EQUAL.

Lessons learned from Positive INFLUENCE

DOCTOR OF RELIGIOUS SCIENCE **Dr. Sunday** IS A HEAVEN ON EARTH EDUCATOR,

'RIGHTEOUSLY COMBATING MADNESS' **bull-riding winner.**

'ALWAYS WAS AND ALWAYS WILL BE' GOD Holy Spirit' (EOE) <u>is</u> The **Positive Spirit** = **without gender.**

= END OF DAZE ON BORROWED TIME =

There's no misinterpreting 'Meaning'

♪ COME TOGETHER RIGHT NOW, OVER ME.

(3)

Does God intervene in human affairs? (PART ONE)

FAITH FORUM

WAR AND REMEMBRANCE *Great Getaways*

legacy TO PAVING THE WAY FOR MY COMING INTO THIS WORLD!
(WW2,ENGLAND.)
WHERE MY STATIONED IN ENGLAND FATHER, A U.S.
AIR FORCE OFFICER, AND A GENTLEMAN'; MET MY BRITISH
MOTHER AT A DANCE; STARTED DATING AND GOT MARRIED.
'SO THEN ON HONEYMOON NIGHT THEY GOT A HOTEL ROOM ON
THE OTHER SIDE OF TOWN, AND WERE ABOUT TO SETTLE IN
FOR THE EVENING WHEN MY MOTHER STATED TO MY FATHER.
I, FORGOT ONE OF MY SUITCASES. 'SO MY GRACIOUS
FATHER, A SOLID CITIZEN GAVE IT THE OL' HONEYMOON NIGHT ?
'WE AIN'T LEFT YET! - SO WHEN THEY RETURNED TO THEIR
HOTEL THAT SAME EVENING; ONLY TO FIND OUT THAT IT WAS
'HITLER AIR BOMB BLOWN TO SMITHEREENS,
AND EVERYBODY IN THE BUILDING WAS KILLED...
IN CONCLUSION: THIS IS WHERE THE LEGENDARY ROOTS OF THIS
MISSION FROM GOD **Step by Step** RELIGION ACTUALLY GOT STARTED!·

FAITH FORUM

Does God intervene in human affairs? (PART TWO)

ANSWERS TO: BY WAY OF 'PRECISION STRING PULLING'
:PARALLEL PHENOMENA:

YOURS TRULY, A CHRISTMAS BABY? I WAS BORN OF A VIRGIN; FOR MY MOTHER WAS ONCE A
VIRGIN. FURTHERMORE, RUMOR HAS IT THAT I WAS DELIVERED BY A STORK! - MY PEDIATRIC
DOCTOR'S LAST NAME WAS STORK. I CAME INTO THIS WORLD AS A 7 MONTH,PREMATURE BABY.
BORN A <u>LIBRA</u> SCALE BRAIN LEFTY. IMMANENTLY, "<u>COMPATIBLE TO ALL</u>" 'A MULTICULTURAL
BLUE EYED, 'HISPANIC—ARAB—JEW' WHO FREQUENTS PIZZA; MAKES THE BEST CHOP SUEY
THIS SIDE OF CHINA. DRINKS SOCIALLY AMEN.' AND VOCALLY HAS BEEN GIVEN A POWER R&B
SINGERS VOICE TO AMUSE -ALL TO UNIFY PEOPLE TO ACCEPT ME AS BEING 'ONE OF THEIRS·

(THE REALISTIC REALITY OF 'PEACE ON EARTH' IS A <u>ONE WORLD RELIGION</u> "ONLY TRUTH CAN FREE YOU"
'REVOLUTIONARY CRUNCH TIME' OR SAME OLD STORY - DIFFERENT DAY! ♫ IMAGINE ALL THE PEOPLE LIVING
LIFE AS --- A MAN HAS GOT TO KNOW HIS "<u>SAME PAGE</u>" RELIGIOUS LIMITATIONS; OR THE WHOLE WORLD
AS IS, REMAINS A STATUS QUO, CALAMITY)...

The art of restoring magnetic heads

"ALL GOD'S CHILDREN, HISTORIC INAUGURAL DECLARATION"

TAKEOFF POINT ♫ MEET THE NEW BOSS' '<u>NOT</u> THE SAME AS THE OLD BOSS.

only **ONE** UNIVERSAL **GOD** Bless you. <u>The</u> <u>Positive</u> *SPIRIT* Without *GENDER*.

'writing revolution' Another world is possible!'

The world is waiting, Inquiring Minds Want to Know: (4)

Writer traces roots of religion

Should you study other religions before adopting one?

THE GOSPEL ACCORDING TO RELIGION & POLITICS is

A PRODUCT OF A **SUPERCONNECTED** MAN, AND <u>HIS</u> **GOD.**

exemplifies What you need to know **AND** Process.

THE SEARCH FOR SIGNS OF INTELLIGENT LIFE IN THE UNIVERSE ?

2012, SCIENCE DISCOVERY! **'God particle'** Connection

ALL CONTRIBUTING TO A MEDIA **ignored**

1980 *foundation of God's new world* by 'PEN NAME' **DR. Sunday.**

only **ONE** **UNIVERSAL** **GOD** Bless you.

<u>INFORMATION BANK</u>: **GOD** is <u>THE</u>

UNIVERSE LENDER, OMNIPOTENT
SPENDER AND MENDER OF HEART'S
THAT ARE TENDER. PURE LOVE'S
ONE AND ONLY SENDER,.

The Positive *<u>SPIRIT</u>* Without *<u>GENDER</u>*.

"GLOBALLY SPEAKING" SO MANY WOMEN TO
RELIGIOUSLY EMANCIPATE, 'SO LITTLE TIME.

PROPITIOUSLY AN EQUAL OPPERTUNITY EMPLOYER.

"ALL GOD'S CHILDREN, HISTORIC INAUGURAL DECLARATION"

THE `Positive` spirit, **PRESCRIPTION STRENGTH**

WITHIN, **Sheds Light on the Body of the Beholder!**.

Life Lessons as Timeless as Infinity

'ALWAYS WAS AND ALWAYS WILL BE' GOD Holy Spirit' (EOE) is The **Positive Spirit = without gender.**

'WORD ON' LEGENDARY MAVERICK 'PREACHER YOURS TRULY, *Mr. Nice Guy.*

"for I am no better than any human –kind person – in any human-kind situation "

=Speaks volumes.) WALK IN MY SHOES P-L-E-A-S-E ● (5)

Today's, Briefing *Teaching Intelligence,* Apostle Lips Now.'

FAITH FORUM

Is religion moving in right direction?

(((H-E-L-L NO!)))

'NOT WHEN THE DEVIL'S BEEN COAXING PEOPLE TO GO TO
CHURCH AND RECEIVE THE CORONAVIRUS COMMUNION. ☹

FAITH FORUM

Why are young Americans less religious?

YOURS TRULY RESPONSE; THEIR JUST NOT INTO THE DILLY, DALLY, DOGMA,
OR DANCING TO THE BEAT OF THE NEANDERTHAL CHARLESTON!!!

QUOTE PANEL RESPONSE OF "BRIAN E. MELENDEZ; AMERICAN INDIAN SPIRITUALITY
SCHOLAR. IT'S NOT THEIR FAULT; THEY ARE NOT PART OF THAT HISTORY. PERHAPS
'IT WAS NEVER THEIR PURPOSE TO CARRY OUR LEGACY? MOREOVER, THEY'VE BEEN
TASKED TO CREATE SOMETHING ELSE: OUR FUTURE". THUS YOURS TRULY RESPONSE,
`FURTHERMORE ANSWERS TO: 'TAKE YOU TO ME LEADER'...

FAITH FORUM

Is religion a barrier to gender equality?

(((ALWAYS HAS BEEN)))

Get 'er done: Pass the Equal Rights Amendment now

FAITH FORUM

Do religions update sex policies?

'THIS ONE'S GOT ALL THE ~~BASES~~ BEDROOMS COVERED...

FAITH FORUM   "AS WAS STATED BY HILLARY CLINTON"   USA TODAY – RENO GAZETTE-JOURNAL
SATURDAY, MAY 27, 2017   & YOURS TRULY.

What is your biggest fear?

Clinton: Free society at risk when truth is under attack

– THE MOST OVER-RATED AND INSULTING STATEMENT IS THAT – "WE'RE ALL IN THIS TOGETHER".
IN TRYING TO CON'VINCE THE DESOLATE HOMELESS, ALONG WITH ALL THE ONE'S WITHOUT
HEALTH-CARE ETC; OF THE VALIDITY OF THIS STATEMENT?! – AND 'YOU'LL BE OUR NEXT PRES-
IDENT!!! REALITY CHECK, FOR ALL THOSE OPPRESSED PEOPLE OUT THERE; 'THE PURSUIT OF
HAPPYNESS IS NOTHING BUT A 'CON - - - STITUTION... – SUNDAY

= FRYER FLYER =
NEWSLETTERCOMMENTARY
'BYTHEMONKAMONGYOU'
Stories that spark a thousand more.
'LITERARY RELOAD!
'WELCOME TO ROBOT SCHOOL,
WITH THIS CURE-ALL CONTAGIOUS
PRAYER OF THE UNIQUE HOMOSAPIENS. ☺

- GOT PEACE??? A LOOK BACK AT THIS 'CONFLICTUAL SHOWSTOPPER PRAYER!!!
WHEREAS, WE'RE 'ALL ONE IN THE SAME PEOPLE RESPONSIBLE FOR THE SAFETY
AND WELL BEING OF 'ALL PEOPLE... CHART YOUR COURSE TO A BETTER
IMPROVEMENT OF 'PERSONAL' HISTORY...

DO YOU SUPPORT
FREEDOM OF speech,
For THIS Voice of The Voiceless?
New book tells of
WE'RE NOT GONNA TAKE IT ANYMORE BEGINS HERE.
on your side Help fight back against
aims to 'revitalize' society
experience a renaissance
LETTUCE **PREY.**

(6)

FAITH IN THE TIME OF COVID-19

according to DR.SUNDAY.

Inevitable option read:

IT'S YOUR CALL.

How `His scriptures view

- AT 'THIS CORONAVIRUS DATE AND TIME'
ONE DOSEN'T HAVE TO GATHER WITH THE
MASSES FOR PRAYER.'GOD HEAR'S YOUR
PRAYERS EVEN IF YOUR JUST AT HOME
PEELING POTATOES...

"AT THIS PANDEMIC IN TIME; 'I BELIEVE IN DISTANCE LEARNING'
HOME SCHOOL COMPUTER, ETC. 'STAYING ALIVE IS AN EDUCATION
WITHIN ITSELF'. GRADUATE ON THAT". $EDUCATION IN THE
FAST LANE, (VS) PARTY ANIMALS ON HIATUS!!! 'LET'S GIVE
IT A YEAR...

INTRODUCING: THE CORONAVIRUS BIRTHDAY CAKE! THAT'S WHERE YOU BLOW OUT 'ALL THE
CANDLES; AND CAUSE OF THE VIRUS SPREADING GERM 'POTENTIAL; YOU GET TO HAVE YOUR
CAKE AND EAT IT TOO. ‿

Protect
yourself

Don't
FORGET!

NOBODY ASKED ME BUT

'COVID-19 IS STILL A TEENAGER.

Where There's A GOD All Mighty Will,

We Are All Connected !

A PROMISE FULFILLED

DELIVERS.

Answers to Mysterious

End of an age, **Prophecy Fulfilled:**

STEP BY STEP, *A Whole New*

Constitutional freedom *Phenomenon.*

PACKAGE FOR **When Hell Turned to Heaven**

with PROPOSED REFORMS *That Will Blow You Away!*

UNIVERSAL **Faith** Reformation

Greatest show on Earth campaign !

BIG-TIME INSPIRATION

'RIGHTEOUSLY COMBATING MADNESS'

Come on inside!

Celebrate America

AMERICAN WRITERS INSTITUTE PROUDLY PRESENTS

journalist Release of

C H R O N I C L E S (7)

Get ready for truth support

NOBODY SHOULD BE LEFT OUT OF

'TELLING IT LIKE IT IS DEMOCRACY'

IN AMERICA speaking out On Controversial Issues?

The future of VOICE YOUR OPINIONS

"IN REPRESENTING AMERICA IT'S IMPORTANT TO HAVE VARYING POLITICAL POINTS OF VIEW." **EFFECTIVE DIVERSIFICATION** matters.

YOURS TRULY SIGNED, Customer SERVICE Representative for

The voters nobody seems to know.

Based on Notebooks 'Plan for Prosperity'

As Book lovers gear up for sale

ALL THE YEARS OF COVER-UP!

FOR THE RECORD Once Upon A Time,

(WILL REMAIN Anonymous)

Who Knew What, and When?

"Pardons DESIGN To Rule."

Political GUARANTEE, Talk show host,

NATION-WIDE *Letters to the Editor* ETC,

THAT NEVER GOT ANY RESPONSE.

Intro of - The LEGEND Of ANYWHERE but Here FREE Speech:

of presentation, "Let freedom truly reign." (8)

Will COVID-19 strengthen or weaken religion?

- THIS -
BECOMES A 'SPIRITUAL AWAKENING' ALONG WITH 'CLIMATE CHANGE'.

We all have a role in saving the world..

THE DEVASTATING EFFECTS OF THE 'WAR OF THE COLD SHOULDER'./

'stories from front lines'
resolution zero homelessness.

NEXT PAGE FOLLOW-UP = = =

The shape of things to come

Should we reinterpret scriptures with changing times?

- THAT'S WHAT 'THIS BOOK'S NEW AGE RELIGIOUS REFORMATION' IS ALL ABOUT.

Echos *of the* past

How can religions help women to break the glass ceiling?

"BY WAY OF HANDING THEM THIS HERE BOOK IN BRICK FORM,
TO BREAK ON THROUGH TO THE OTHER SIDE"...

Women's soccer and the equal pay debate

Call Time Out!

I'M A BIG FAN OF WOMEN'S SOCCER; BUT I'D NEED TO DO ATLEAST AN HR'S LONG
'VERBAL' TV PRESENTION TO PUT THIS DEBATE IN PERSPECTIVE. THEREFORE, ALL THIS
- BECOMING A PART OF -

first steps into democracy

'social distancing'
... Making the case ...
Words of wisdom Showstoppers.

"IT'S BETTER TO BE 6FT APART, THAN IT IS TO BE 6FT UNDER".

ON THE FRONT LINES

- IN COMBATING THIS ISSUE; JUST 'SALUTE EACH OTHER FROM A 6 FOOT DISTANCE,
BEING A TOUCH-LESS SAFE WAY TO ACKNOWLEDGE EACH OTHER, AND STILL'
HAVING THIS FEELING OF CONNECTION!!!

'HOW IT ALL GOT STARTED' - THIS SOUNDS FAMILIAR!
- IT ALL STARTED IN CHINA; WHERE DURING A ROCK CONCERT; A
CHINESE ROCK STAR STANDING IN A GIANT PETRIDISH, LITERALLY
BIT THE HEAD OFF OF A BAT.. ‿"

How should we handle materialism?
FAITH FORUM   (REVOLUTIONARY PREACHER WITH BOOK IN THE WORKS)

FROM THE 'GET GO' THE REASON I DON'T WEAR JEWELRY, IS BECAUSE I'M A SALESMAN
FOR GOD, AND NOT A JEWELRY SALESMAN! 'I HAVE NO DESIRE FOR ANY MATERIAL VANITY
TRINKETS OR EXTRAVAGENT WEALTH. FEED ME, CAR ME (2) HEALTH CARE ME, AND I'M
GOOD TO GO. - GIVE ME A HEAVY DUTY MAID SERVICE ONCE A WEEK FOR MY STUDIO APT;
AND I'M A HAPPY CAMPER, LIVING IN THIS MY MAN-CAVE MANSION. ("UPON MY SUCCESS")
I COULD USE A STATE OF THE ART OFFICE. 'MONEY AIN'T FOR NOTHING' AND THE CHAR-
ITIES ARE ALL MENT TO BE! - OTHER THAN FOUNDATION UP-KEEP, AND EMPLOYEE PAYROLL.
= 'MY FAVORITE CHARITY WOULD BE TO BUILD WHOLE COMMUNITIES OF TINY LITTLE HOUSES
FOR THE HOMELESS' THUS ALL BECOMING A 'THINK YOURSELF OUT OF THE BOX' VILLAGE.

"STOP THE WORLD 'I, WANT TO GET ON."
'WELCOME TO STATIONS OF THE DOUBLE-CROSSED'.

ALL GOD'S CHILDREN "COMMON FOLK" DELIVERANCE!!!

REMEMBER: ONLY 'YOU CAN PREVENT OLIGARCHY! STATUS QUO ENDORSED CHRISTIANITY, IS A
GLORIFIED ONE HERO RELIGION IN 'JESUS'; AS FOR THE REST OF US BARGANLESS 'NOBODYS'
- NEED NOT BE ASKING FOR ANYTHING, NOR BE EXPECTING ANYTHING. SIGNED: PSYCHO-OLOGY.
'A PENNY FOR YOUR THOUGHTS...

T-H-E-R-E-F-O-R-E VOTE 'CRY WOLF' REFORM.

'THIS HERE GOD INSTILLED FORMULA'
has never been so important.

👍Like "UNTILL THERE'S 'FREE MEDICAL FOR 'ALL (MEDICARE?) - AND 'FREE EDUCATION
FOR ALL THE QUALIFYING PROFESSIONAL MEDICAL STAFF, AMEN". - THAN YOU CAN
CLAIM AS LIKE IN THE MOVIE, 'GREED IS GOOD'...

(Message is Forever.)

(10)

READING REVOLUTION

"Storytelling on a grand scale"

HISTORY ON DISPLAY

BY Founder of 'THE POSITIVE Faith 'ONE WORLD' Religion.

👍 **The world according to** DR . SUNDAY.

expanding intellectually FEATURES

Wit&Wisdom AMAZING VIEWS

News, notes, quips & quotes

Observations, confessions and revelations

Vintage Journalism REVIEW & **TAKEOFF POINT** ●

TIME CAPSULE Calendar of Events

STORY-LINE 1980 ,. *featuring* CONSECUTIVE YEARS!

Religious Science training program ☞

Crime & Punishment ☞ PAGE (62)

WAR AND REMEMBRANCE ☞ PAGE (82)

Tha Birds & Tha Bees ☞ PAGE (94)

"That was tha week that was". ☞ PAGE (109)

Up to tha Challenge, Sportsline :

A **look back**

- ASK NOT WHAT 'YOU ASSUME AND OR WANT TO ASSUME, OF GOD'S EXPECTATIONS OF YOU; 'BUT WHAT GOD'S EXPECTATIONS OF 'YOU ACTUALLY ARE. - AS YOU WILL FIND IN THIS HERE FORETELLING BOOK! IN TAKING MY MANIFESTO OUT FOR A TEST DRIVE; 'I LOVE THE SMELL OF REVOLUTION IN THE MORNING... (11)

VALIDATION TIME FOR

What is your most powerful argument to prove God's existence?

Media frenzy, fly on the wall taped interviews anyone?

Making the case
Need a new roommate?

FAITH FORUM   Sunday, November 13, 2016

Does God speak directly to humans?

INFLUENCED

God told me to   In Testimony Whereof

Divine inspiration **INVISIBLE GUIDING**

INNERSOUL SUPPORT SYSTEM.   **POWER OF ONE**

'**THE** POSITIVE SPIRIT,

Holy GHOSTWRITER

GOD

OF

MOSES .

The
Positive SPIRIT,
long reach:

---AND THEN SOME...

RENO GAZETTE-JOURNAL   **FAITH FORUM**   SUNDAY, MARCH 30, 2014

What is the formula for happiness?

•ACCOUNTABILITY.

IN BRIEF: PERSONAL 'ACCOMPLISHMENTS' IN EVERYDAY LIFE RESULTING
FROM 'ONE'S OWN HARMONIOUS P-O-S-I-T-I-V-E CONTRIBUTIONS".

BEST *formula for* GOT GOD?.

(12)

What makes a good sermon?

word choice matters

Religious Science INDUSTRY OF

Positive

INFLUENCE

BEST OF THE BEST

'WELCOME TO SERMON CITY'

"FEATURING THE POSITIVE SPIRIT, GHOSTWRITER"

"PEACE ON EARTH STARTS WITH INDIVIDUAL HALO'ISM;
WHEREAS TRUE 'POSITIVE MORAL MENTORING CAN RESULT IN
BECOMING THE PRECISIAN DRUG, ONE NEVER COMES DOWN FROM"...

- YOURS TRULY RESPONSE TO: "POPE FRANCIS MADE AN EXTREMELY
CONTROVERSIAL STATEMENT THE OTHER DAY.
HE SAYS HE BELIEVES ANYONE CAN
GO TO HEAVEN IF YOU DO GOOD DEEDS, EVEN ATHEISTS!" - EXCEPT
WHEN YOU GET TO HEAVEN AND "YOU WANT TO GO TO 'THEIR BASE BALL'
WORLD SERIES; THEY ALWAYS PUT YOU GUYS UP IN THE NOSE BLEED SECTION. ☺

2020 WINGIN' IT

AT THE CONFESSIONAL:

BLESS ME FATHER FOR I HAVED SINNED; FATHER MY LAST CONFESSION WAS
BACK IN 1959!! (TRUE STORY) I ASKED SOME GAL IN THE BAR LAST WEEKEND;
'SO WHAT'S YOUR ETHNIC BACKROUND? - AND SHE RESPONDED TO ME, THAT SHE'S
A DENTAL HYGIENEST; SO THAN 'I ORDERED WHAT 'SHE WAS DRINKING!! 'SEEING
HOW THAT I'M THE MESSIAH, AND IN RETAINING MY TITLE; I BETTER NOT BE HERE TO LONG FATHER...

What is the 'proper' way to interpret scriptures?

"AN EXAMPLE: PRAYER, AS WAS ONCE WRITTEN: LEAD US 'NOT INTO TEMPTATION; BUT DELIVER US FROM
EVIL AMEN" • MEANING WHAT!!! 'DELIVER US FROM COMBAT WITH FRANKENSTEIN AMEN??? 'TOO INEPT'
((VS) YOURS TRULY, TAKE! 'LEAD US 'NOT INTO TEMPTATION; BUT DELIVER US FROM 'EVER BECOMING'
EVIL AMEN... 'MAKES FOR BEING 'PRAYER OF THE CONQUERUING ANGEL...

"ALWAYS REMEMBER, EVERYTIME A CASH REGISTER BELL RINGS
FROM THE PURCHASE OF THIS BOOK, AN ANGEL GETS THEIR WINGS."

A way into the system aims to 'revitalize' society

"My fellow American **whistleblowers** the only thing we have to "fear" is the lack of significant free-speech, or realistic democracy."

'NATIONWIDE LETTERS TO THE EDITOR' FAITH BASED INITIATIVE; 'MEDIA BANNED—Vintage Journalism'

2018 "PRESIDENT TRUMP, STRONGLY APPROVED OF 'FAITH BASED INITIATIVE" •
SAM! TO BOASTFULLY CLAIM TO HAVE PUT A MAN ON THE MOON, WITHOUT EVER CLAIMING TO HAVE PUT A MAN ON PHENOMENAL HEAVEN ON EARTH, IS ABSURD!!! "FIRST MAN" IN The art of restoring magnetic heads.

Justice Dept. 'all in' on criminal justice reform

"ANARCHIES FINEST HOUR"

LIVING IN A SOCIETY WHERE THE BEST WAY TO GET BACK AT AND UN-EMPLOY ALL THOSE RUTHLESS POLICE OFFICERS, ALONG WITH ALL THE HIGHFALUTIN' PEOPLE WORKING IN THE COURT SYSTEM, IS TO 'B-E-H-A-V-E = Y-O-U-R-S-E-L-F' AND THAT'LL HURT'EM OHO SO BIG TIME IN THEIR POCKET BOOKS; ARE YOU G-A-M-E EVERYONE???

EXPERIENCE HAVING A BEAUTIFUL MIND.

VICTIM'S OUTRAGE

'RELATIVE TO ALL RELATIVES' INJUSTICE IS UNSOLVED CRIME, WHEREAS THE VICTIM'S DO INSURMOUNTABLE TIME, FOR EVERY FORM OF CRIME IS INJUSTICE STATE OF MIND, IT'S PEOPLE BORN OF GOOD INTENSIONS THAT NEVER SEEM TO RHYME, TO WALK A CROOKED ROAD IN LIFE; IS A LIFE OF WASTED TIME...

C H R O N I C L E S

Questionnaire – Press Release Essential

5. Who are the main characters and why are they important to the story?

RIGHT FROM WRONG, GOOD FROM EVIL, ON RELIGION? GIVE ME 'ALL YOUR FLUNKIES! YOU DON'T NEED A WAFER COMMUNION TO BE IN SYNC WITH THIS CRACKER. A MAN HAS GOT TO KNOW 'HIS SAME PAGE RELIGIOUS LIMITATIONS, OR THE WHOLE WORLD JUST ALL BECOMES A 'GO TO HELL SOCIETY! — AS LIKE IN AL-QAIDA'S 'DOGMA, ETC, ETC, IT'S ALL JUST FOAMING AT THE MOUTH...

TO ALL MY RELIGIOUS COMPETITORS "WHEN YOUR DOGMA QUITS BARKING FREEDOM OF CHOICE' IS FOR YOU TO PREACH 'MY GOSPEL AND KEEP ALL YOUR $$$ PARISHIONERS, OR SUFFER THE CONSEQUENCES OF HEAVY DUTY COMPETITION.

"IN BRIEF: *Life according to* **a new modern**

DAY RELIGIOUS CLEAN SLATE." (14)

1980 *foundation of God's new world* by 'PEN NAME' **DR. Sunday.**

THE GOSPEL ACCORDING TO RELIGION & POLITICS
A PRODUCT OF A **SUPERCONNECTED** MAN, AND <u>HIS</u> **GOD.**

THIS HERE BOOK IS DEDICATED TO THE ONE AND ONLY, ALWAYS WAS AND ALWAYS WILL BE, 'POSITIVE MIRACLE WORKING GOD! SIGNED: ALL GOD'S CHILDREN...

News, notes, quips & quotes

Observations, confessions and revelations

AMAZING VIEWS

STORY—REVEALING—ESSAYS.

Printed in the United States of America
Publisher: Dr. Sunday's Religious and Political Views.

"ALL NEWSPAPER FONTS ETC; IN THIS HERE BOOK ARE USED FOR ILLISTRATIVE CREATION FROM 'MY OWN' WORDED TAKE ON THESE HERE STORIES, AND OR IN 'MOST CASES BITS AND PIECES, TOTALLY IRRELEVANT TO THE INITIAL HEADLINE 'STORY FONT THAT IT CAME FROM. THEREFORE USABLE FONTS, WHEREAS ALLOT OF THESE ILLUSTRATIONS IN THIS HERE BOOK ARE NOTHING MORE THEN A BUNCH OF MONA LISA'S WITH MUSTACHES!" - ALONG WITH 'MY ORIGINAL DRAWINGS...

WRITTEN BY YOURS TRULY, DR. SUNDAY

TAKING STOCK OF statements put on paper

Art is whatever an artist says it is.

'KEEP CURSIVE HAND WRITING IN OUR SCHOOLS! WHEREAS NOBODY WILL EVER GET THE CHANCE TO FORG SOMEONE ELSES X, ON YOUR CHECK...

IN READING THIS GRASSROOTS <u>MANUSCRIPT</u> "ON ALL <u>(RELIGIOUSLY EDITED PAGES)</u> OF THIS HERE BOOK!" THIS WORD "THE" IS ALWAYS IN DIRECT, OR INDIRECT REFERENCE TO GOD. THIS WORD "THA" IS ALWAYS IN DIRECT, OR INDIRECT REFERENCE TO MAN.

TELLING IT LIKE IT IS

((EXAMPLE) WE ARE 'THA LITTLE EXTENSIONS, FROM 'THE BIG EXTENDER; 'NOT LITTLE gods. (15)

END OF AN ERA

'STARTING OVER! - COMING OUT OF THE DARK AGES - ANYONE?

THE BIBLE & QURAN **ACCORDING TO A** CONCLUSION!

PUBLISHERS CLEARING HOUSE 'TWO FOR ONE CLOSEOUT SALE

Say It Ain't So, Reality Check **Tha Party's Over.** ☺

Bible **Deciphering** reform plan

Time to Rescue *tha* Flintstone Judeo-Christian *Once Upon A Time* Bible'. ETC.

1989. <u>**quote** John Shelby Spong</u>. Episcopal bishop of Newark, New Jersey.

RE-EDITED MUCH "**improved**" **version of** *Written* BY *YOURS TRULY,.*

THA LITTERAL INTERPETATIONS OF THA BIBLE HAVE FOSTERED SOME OF THA MOST HIDEOUS OF INSTITUTIONS SUCH AS WAR AND REVENGE. 'MANY A CASE OF SOLE SEARCHING DELUSIONAL PSYCOTIC CRIME, SUCH AS JIM JONES, OR DAVID KORESH, ETC.' INFERIOR FUROR, OR THA HITLER BIBLE READING COURSE OF 'CHOSEN PEOPLE' ANTI-SEMITISM. THA SUBJUGATION OF WOMEN. HOMOPHOBIA. CONDONATION OF SLAVERY VIA ECONOMIC OPPRESSION. 'A BOOK RESPONSIBLE FOR THESE STATEMENTS THUS INACTMENTS, CANNOT BE IN ANY LITERAL SENSE THE TRUE WORD OF **God.**

'IN THAT THA BIBLE IS ALL IN ALL MORE ANCIENT HUMAN STANDARD CREATED THEN GOD INSPIRED. CONSPICUOUSLY THA BIBLE IS A BOOK OF SYMBOLIC RATHER THEN LITERAL VERSES, OR UNSCIENTIFIC ILLOGICAL HUMAN FABLES TOLD THRU OLD-TIME MORAL PRECEPTS. THEREFORE IN NEED OF LIBERATION FROM ITS OWN TEACHINGS, TO BE UPDATED AND REWRITTEN FOR THA PEOPLE OF OUR TIMES, AND ALL TIMES'...

THE GOSPEL **According to Word Perfect.**

A work of monumental religious and political significance.

PORTRAITS OF EXTRAORDINARY LIVES

CELEBRATING YEARS OF 'NEW STORIES ABOUT OUR MOST OUTSTANDING PEOPLE AND EVENTS: WHAT'S NEW? REAL WORLD BREAKTHROUGH! 'THE BIBLE OF A NEW AGE, GREATEST BOOK EVER WRITTEN; RECOUNTING RESTRUCTURING REWRITING, LIFE STORIES AND REVIEWING WORLD HISTORY. TEAMING UP FOR NEW DISCOVERIES! 'FORMULA TO PROPHECY DECLARED DEAD AWAKEN TO A NEW LIFE. NEWS YOUTH CAN USE: IMAGINE YOURSELF IN 'THE LIVING BIBLE' ANGELES PUT IN RIGHT FIELD, WILL BE UPDATED AND ETERNALLY OPEN; PAYING HOMAGE TO 'ALL' INSPIRATIONAL AND INGENIOUS PROPHETS; CAN ALL BUT GUARANTEE YOUR SPOT ON THE BEST SELLER LIST. 'ANNOUNCING AUTHENTIC BIBLE PROPHECY, "YOU CAN BUY IN" WORLDWIDE RECOGNITION. HISTORY MADE AVAILABLE TO YOU. MAGIC KINGDOM CLUB SPOTLIGHT ON EXTRA BUNDLES! PASSING OF TIME 'SINS' WILL SOON BE FORGIVEN...

(WRITTEN IN 1983, BY YOURS TRULY THA COMMISSIONER.) (16)

MISS ONE page and you miss a lot

Friends for life

"THE MOST HONORABLE LIFE TIME ACHIEVEMENT AWARD IS TO BE 'POSITIVELY RECOGNIZED IN THIS HERE' NEW AGE BIBLE (ANNEX). - WHEREAS, THERE'S PLENTY OF PEOPLE 'THUS EXAMPLES' OUT THERE DURING THE RECENT HURRICANES AND CORONAVIRUS PANDEMIC THAT CONTRIBUTED TO THE HELPLESS, HOPELESS NEEDY; BY WAY OF THEIR CONTRIBUTIONS SUCHAS IN FEEDING AND SHELTERING THEM "ETC" - 'BIG TIME'. LADIES AND GENTLEMAN; THESE ARE 'OUR MODERN DAY SAINTS!!!

IN YOUR CORNER.

CBS NEWS PROMO CONTEST, 'NOTE TO SELF'•
'RECOGNITION TO THOSE'

'BLESSED ARE ALL THE POSITIVE PLUS,
$CHARITABLE GIVERS OF THIS WORLD;

"FOR WITHOUT 'THEM THERE WOULD BE NO GOD'S WORLD".

- WITH THE LIKES OF DOCTORS WITHOUT BOARDERS,
'HABITAT FOR HUMANITY'-"ETC" THUS KUDOS, TO ALL
THE FIRST RESPONDERS! - ALONG WITH ALL THE EXAMPLES
OF 'GOOD DEED DOING' HEARTFELT VOLUNTEERS, IN THIS
HERE A GLOBAL SOCIETY MAKING THIS WORLD
A MORE BEARABLE PLACE TO LIVE., 'RIGHT ON THRU
TO ALL THE PERSON OR PERSONS, THAT WOULD
GIVE YOU THE SHIRT, OR SHIRTS OFF THEIR BACKS!
SIGNED: BEACH BUMS ANONYMOUS. ☺

Food Pantry PHILOSOPHY

HOROSCOPE

Libra (Sept. 23-Oct. 23).

You use what you need and gladly give the rest to others. To you it's not even generosity, really; it's just keeping the resources flowing.
SIGNED:ANONYMOUS...

(17)

Church Directory Viewpoint

" ALL God's Children "

ONLY TRUTH CAN FREE YOU

"Tha whole enchilada"
TIME
Since tha beginning :

THE ALL SEEING,
ALL KNOWING
one and only
GOD
HOLY/POSITIVE
spirit

Jesus Christ,
Bible study <u>Man-</u>
<u>God</u> **imitation** !

'Spiritual Awakening'
"HE DIED FOR HIS SIN"

World must face truth:

FLESH AND BLOOD MAN is ONLY MAN, MAID
iN THA IMAGE AND LiKENESS OF ONESELF.

ANGELS ARE THOSE OF US ON THIS HERE
PLANET EARTH THAT ARE DiLiGENTLY COMMITED
TO SERVING GOD; MAY FiND THEMSELVES FROM
TIME TO TIME HAVING A LiKENESS TOWARDS
EATING CHiCKEN OR TURKEY WINGS.

CLEARED FOR TAKEOFF
FLYING HIGH

ANGELS AMONG US

SPECIAL REPORT

(18)

INFORMATION BANK:

"DECODING THA PARALLELS"
CAPITALIZE ON His positive imagination

'OR NEW KID ON THA BLOCK, (VERSUS) J.C.! 'IN BRIEF'
BORN IN THA VICINITY OF BETHLEHEM STEEL OR FACTORY AIR,
(VS) FACTORY HEIR! RAISED IN THE ORIGINAL SIN CITY, OR HISTORIC
CALUMET CITY, ILL. 5 LETTERS FIRST NAME, 6 LETTERS LAST. I WAS BORN OF A
VIRGIN FOR MY MOTHER WAS ONCE A VIRGIN; WAS THA LION WHO DID AN 8 YEAR
STINT, IN A PAROCHIAL SCHOOL AS A NON-BELIEVER CAT-LICK; WHO'S
CHALLENGING THIS ORIGINAL CATHOLIC., YOURS TRULY, WAS ONCE A SCHOOL
BUS DRIVER AND A PLAYGROUND SUPERVISOR, WHO TAUGHT TRUTHS TO THA CHILDREN OF
NAPERVILLE ; WAS WORKING AS A CARPENTERS HELPER WHEN I OPENED MY FIRST
SAVINGS ACCOUNT. HE DIED AT 33. I STARTED WRITING AT 33., "ALL BY COINCIDENCE".

COMPATIBLE TO "ALL" A LIBRA SCALE BRAIN LEFTY.
== I'M THA SOMEBODY THAT NOBODY CAN ACCEPT, FOR I'M
THA NOBODY THAT WILL SOMEDAY BE ACCEPTED ! THA COACH OF THA HORSES, OR THA
WORK HORSE THAT ISN'T A PHONY. THA LINK THAT'S GOING TO LINE YOU, AND THA LINE
THAT'S GOING TO LINK YOU. ELOQUENTLY BEING THA STAGE WITHIN YOUR WORLD THAT HAS
A GOOD PART FOR EVERYBODY. THA IMAGINATION WE'RE ALL PRODUCTS OF, OR THA POSITIVE
IMAGINATION; PROPHETICALLY THA SEEDED WONDER, THAT SUPERSEDES THA SEEDLESS
WONDER; FOR THEN MAY WE ALL BE SEATED. THA PROPHET THAT BELIEVES IN PROFIT
SHARING. THA SHRINK THAT HAS NO INTENTIONS OF SHRINKING ANYONE, OR THA PILL
YOU CAN ALL TAKE. WHEREFORE I'M THA MONK AMONG YOU, THAT WILL NEVER STOP
MONKEYING AROUND. PERTINACIOUSLY THA SNAKE CHARMER YOU DON'T HAVE TO GRASP
FOR. THA ROCKNE, YOU DON'T HAVE TO KNEE TO; A AMOS ALONZO STAG, PROTEGE TYPE
ALL-AMERICAN. THA LIP TONGUE SENT FROM KRIPTON - WITH TRUTH, JUSTICE, AND
'THE POSITIVE WAY.
= FOR ALL THOSE PARALLELS ARE TRUE, EXCEPT I'M 'NOT
THAT SAME JEW; I'M JUST THA BUD THAT'S WISER.

"I WANT TO LIVE IN A WORLD WHERE THERE'S MORE BUGLERS THEN BURGLARS; WHEREAS
EVERY COWARD HAS A SILVER LINING. APPROPRIATELY MORE HARLEQUINS THEN HOOLIGANS.
I MAY ONLY HAVE A COUPLE OF SKELETONS IN MY CLOSET, BUT ATLEAST I DON'T HAVE
ANY DINOSAUR BONES. I WANT TO LIVE IN A WORLD WHERE THA IRON CLAD FOOT OF
OPPRESSION BECOMES A HUSHPUPPY. U.S. ARMY DRAFTED AND QUALIFIED AS A MARKSMAN
BUT, THA SOLDIER THAT WAS HANDED THA SHARPSHOOTERS MEDAL, BECAUSE THEY RAN OUT
OF MARKS MEN. NEWS MEDIA SIGNED, AND READY FOR THA ALL S-T-A-R-E GAME...

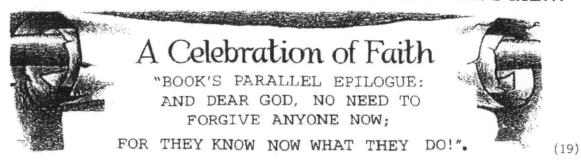

A Celebration of Faith
"BOOK'S PARALLEL EPILOGUE:
AND DEAR GOD, NO NEED TO
FORGIVE ANYONE NOW;
FOR THEY KNOW NOW WHAT THEY DO!".

(19)

Nevada's hidden gem revealed

Dr. Sunday show

On record **2001** YOURS TRULY (SHOW) PROPOSAL

(((SERMON CITY CATHEDRAL)))

SERMON CITY, <u>PROJECT PROPOSAL</u> TO BECOMING RENO'S `BEST OVER-ALL TOURIST ATTRACTION!!!

'TOSS IN THA NEVADA CEMETERY, EVILDOER PROJECT PROPOSAL'

'AN ALL GOD'S CHILDREN ACCEPT ALL'

TELEVISION MINISTRY *TAPE* Live from Reno

"STATEMENT 'SEPERATION OF CHURCH AND STATE' IS NOT FOUND IN THA CONSTITUTION".

A different kind of church discover where you fit in

PLAN ON RECORD-BREAKING TELEVISION.

WHAT'S IN STORE? WATCH HIM RISE FROM THA DEAD, MASSIVE AUDIENCES OF 'BORED AGAIN CHRISTIANS' *THAT WERE BORED TO DEATH, WITH STATEMENTS LIKE "IF I'M VIRTUALLY HONEST ENOUGH TONIGHT, I SHOULD BE ABLE TO END FREEDOM OF SPEACH!"* NOTE: 'THA=MAN, 'THE=GOD...

THE GOSPEL ACCORDING TO RELIGION & POLITICS

A PRODUCT OF A **SUPERCONNECTED** MAN, AND <u>HIS</u> **GOD.**

Time to Rescue *tha* NEANDERTHAL DISCRIMINATORY *Once Upon A Time Bible'* ETC, ETC.

A work of monumental religious and political significance.

FOR 'ALL' INSPIRATIONAL AND INGENIOUS PROPHETS; <u>WILL BE UPDATED AND ETERNALLY OPEN;</u>

REWRITTEN FOR THA PEOPLE OF OUR TIMES, AND ALL TIMES'...

'FORMULA TO PROPHECY DECLARED DEAD AWAKEN TO A NEW LIFE. SIGNED: *THA COMMISSIONER*

programs promote variety
DON'T UNDERESTIMATE PAGE 18.

Get ready for fantastic shows. *PROGRAMING:*

What's Up Doc? PODIUM SEGMENT. WEEKLY NEWS & REVIEW, ACCORDING TO AUTHOR'S CREDENTIALS. ((COMEDY SEGMENT.)) TRUCK LOADS OF YOURS TRULY WRITTEN SKITS, ACTING WITH GUEST. ((FATHER THYME, COOKING SEGMENT.)) OVER-ALL SPECIALTY COOKING ALONG WITH OPEN HOUSE CONTEST BY YOURS TRULY, WITH GUEST. ((MUSIC SEGMENT.)) = AN OCCASIONAL BRING DOWN THA HOUSE AND SENATE, ROCK 'N ROLL = BLUES SINGING `BY YOURS TRULY.

story REFLECTION Meter Is Running[20].

The Book That Reveals
The Whole Shocking Truth

Looking to pound home a message.

IS ANYBODY OUT THERE

Disgusted with politics as usual?

on representation **Who Counts, & Who Don't?**

HAD ENOUGH
FEATURES

"Atrocities of Democracy."

WE'VE COME A LONG WAY
SINCE CHARIOT RACING.

WHERE WE ARE NOW

The Secret History **of** Plutocracy

(Government by the Rich.) — THAT IN ITSELF BEING
$TAX-PAYER EXTORTION!!!

versus

The Second Coming
of Democracy
FACTORY TO YOU!

The Untold Stories

The Muzzling OF the Press

You can be a part of mending this! (21)

"My Fellow Americans" Campaign ANNOUNCEMENTS

'IN FORMULATING A PRESIDENTAL EXPLORATORY COMMITTEE ON A <u>MENIAL INCOME</u>, I WENT TO THE PUB, BOUGHT THE HOUSE A ROUND, AND TOLD THEM ABOUT MY ENDEAVOR, AND THEY ALL TOLD ME TO GO FOR IT; SO THEN I ORDERED THEM A SECOND ROUND, AND 'THEN THEY ALL TOLD ME THAT I, WAS GOING TO BECOME A TWO TERM PRESIDENT. :

EFFECTIVE DIVERSIFICATION matters. 'rhetoric of Campaign 20/20

SOPHISTICATED. REFINED. FEARLESS.

"IN THIS CORNER ♫ 'THE REAL LIFE' ROCKY BALBOA OF PRESIDENTIAL POLITICS ♫ —I'LL HIT THEM WITH A POLITICAL LEFT, I'LL HIT THEM WITH A POLITICAL RIGHT, ON AND ON ETC. ETC." story BRIEFING

'LIBERTARIAN' (**Third party**) Independent Lion party presidential candidate.

'I'LL BE 'LION' TO YOU ALL THE TIME! I 'GURU' UP ON POLITICS...

'LABELED BY SOME, TO FUNNY TO BECOME PRESIDENT.

Americans still want people of faith as leaders .

GOSPEL ACCORDING TO 'YOU CAN'T HANDLE THE TRUTH .

– JUDGMENT DAY ON RACISM!!!

The art of restoring magnetic heads – People, to be a card carrying
'HOORAY FOR OUR SIDE' **member of the '<u>true family of God</u>, there are no ethnical differences; whereas people come in all kinds of colors, shapes and sizes; be nice to them'<u>all</u>. One 'mind' fits 'all.**

"PATRIOTISM IS THE BACKBONE OF OUR COUNTRY'
YOURS TRULY, BEST RESTORER OF"

– LEADERSHIP WRITTEN BY A –
'NO WOODEN NICKLES TAKING CONSERATIVE;
HEART OF GOLD PROGRESSIVE; "LIBERTARIAN".

'PEN NAME'
SIGNED: YOURS TRULY, **Dr. Sunday.** (1980) <u>FOUNDER OF THE</u> INAUGURAL FUTURITY OF 'ALL GOD'S CHILDREN' <u>POSITIVE FAITH</u> <u>ONE-WORLD RELIGION</u>. <u>REFORMATION</u> PROGRAM.

THE GOSPEL ACCORDING TO RELIGION & POLITICS

A PRODUCT OF A **SUPERCONNECTED** MAN, AND HIS GOD.

"Always was and always will be God, <u>is</u> The positive spirit without gender."
- IN TEACHING PEOPLE HOW TO BECOME 'FRANK WITHOUT THE BUN. *"for I am no better than any human kind person in any human kind situation"* Speaks volumes.

WANTED
New leader, new nation, new world
'READ HIM AND WEEP'

' issue Briefing' FACTS ON FILE
by A UNIQUE SOURCE of SUPERIOR WISDOM,
that aims to 'revitalize' society.
THE ADVENTURE BEGINS HERE.

THE PRIORITY OF $EDUCATION IS THAT OF BEING A MORALLY PRINCIPLED ONE...

" 'SCHOOLED IN BIG GOTCHA' THE WORDS SEPARATION OF CHURCH AND STATE, ARE NOT FOUND IN THE CONSTITUTION. **"**

'GIVING VALIDATION TO THE STATEMENT 'IN GOD WE TRUST'...

'YOURS TRULY, CAMPAIGN SLOGAN - 'WELCOME TO CIVILIZATION:

"My opinion ON "

 TARIFFS: INFLATION IS QUALITY OF LIFE'S WORST WORST NIGHTMARE! (EXAMPLE) WHEREAS, ALL THE UP-GRADES THE MINIMUM WAGERS HAVE ATTAINED, GO RIGHT BACK TO SQUARE ONE...

ROE (VS) WADE: PLANNED PARENTHOOD (VS) PLANED COAT HANGER! 'PRO-LIFE, GOES INTO EFFECT THE DAY (PRO-INTELLIGENCE, BIRTH CONTROL, COMES OF AGE!) "LIVING IN A AFTER THE FACT SOCIETY WE NEED TO CATCH THIS BEFORE THERE'S A FACT;'CHOOSE PRO-INTELLIGENCE BIRTH CONTROL.

MARIJUANA: 100% BEHIND MEDICAL. - RECREATIONAL? - ONLY FOR PING, PONG, PLAYERS!!! ☺

BORDER CRISIS: "IN BRIEF" I'D MAKE MEXICO THE 51ST STATE. 'KEEP THE BORDER CLOSED FOR THE NEXT 4 YEARS, WHILE WE MOVE IN TO SET UP SHOP. 'DECLARE ENGLISH AS OUR OFFICIAL SPEAKING LANGUAGE, AND SAME CURRENCY. A WIN, WIN, FOR BOTH SIDES. A KINDER, GENTLER, DRUG CARTEL. - ALONG WITH PROFESSIONAL SPORTS TEAMS EXPANSION. ETC, ETC, ETC.

HEALTH CARE: - WITH THE GOVERNMENT'S LACK OF SYMMETRY; WE'RE ALL THAT MUCH CLOSER TO THE CEMETERY! - "TO BE CONTINUED" - EINSTEIN, OR EDISON, WE'RE ALL THE SAME MEDICINE...

(MEDIA QUESTION); ARE YOU JUST ANOTHER DEMOCRATIC SOCIALIST??? 'I'M THE CAPITALIST THAT BELIEVES WE CAN 'ALL CAPITALIZE TOGETHER! THE 'PROPHET' THAT BELIEVES IN 'PROFIT SH-ARING'; - OR THE MORE INDUSTRIES I CAN CONVERT TO THIS IDEOLOGY; - FREE HEALTH CARE, BECOMES THE PAY-OFF OUT COME, OF THIS SO CALLED 'PROFIT SHARING!!!

GLOBAL WARMING: YOURS TRULY MAVERICK PRESIDENTIAL CANDIDATE; WILL TELL YOU TO TOSS INTO THE EQUATION 'OVER-POPULATION' -'AMERICA, 'EVERYTIME YOUR IN A RIDICULUS TRAFFIC JAM; I WANT YOU TO KEEP REPEATING TO YOURSELF; I'M GOING TO VOTE FOR DR. SUNDAY...

" THERE IS NO SUCH THING AS OVER-POPULATION AND 'PIECE ON EARTH' THE MORE THE SCARIER **"**..

hellish conditions. Earth in danger :
TIME SENSITIVE

- WITH ALL THE ON GOING EFFECTS OF 'CLIMATE CHANGE' HAPPENING;
IT'S NOW LIKE TELLING YOUR CHILDREN; - SORRY KID'S; WE GAVE
AWAY ALL OF YOUR ENVIRONMENTAL INHERITANCE TO THE DEVIL...

TRUTH TO POWER

"Open Season on Common Folk Citizens"
Americans are fed up with Calling for Justice,
And wonder; Where can I be safe?
`Resistance must be heard.'
"Atrocities of Democracy."
Imagemakers "stop this cover-up!"
Another world is possible!'

"THE TIME IS HERE. THE TIME IS NOW. THIS IS THE MOMENT."

'IT'S THE CURRICLUM STUPID'.

☞ IN CRIME PREVENTION'KNOWLEDGE IS SAFETY.

2ND AMENDMENT : "PEOPLE KILL PEOPLE; GUNS DON'T KILL PEOPLE".

'MENTAL HEALTH-CARE VIA 'POSITIVE INFLUENCE' SAVES LIVES;

'YOURS TRULY, THE BEST ON THE PLANET AT DISHING THIS OUT IN VOLUMES.

TO MAKE'UM THINK, IS TO MAKE'UM BLINK!

(((TRUE TO LIFE)))

'WHEREAS THIS HERE BEING A GAME WINNING 'MINDFUL INTERCEPTION
OF A POTENTIAL EVIL DOERS ONSLAUGHT...

'ON A MISSION FROM GODZILLA; WAKE-UP CALL, ACTION-STOPPER.
REVITALIZING NEW-AGE 'SET YOU STRAIGHT' CURRICULUM ANYONE?

"My opinion will change how people think and behave ;
ALL CONTRIBUTING TO A **contagious-philosophy."**

THE DAY AFTER

'MYSTIC NOMORE; EVIL' NOT FOOLING ANYONE WHEN WE KNOW JUST HOW THEY THINK! = FURTHERMORE =
- WITH ALL MY PROPOSALS TO THIS HERE SENSITIVE ISSUE BEING DENIED ACCESS TO THE PUBLIC 'BY
THE 1%ERS - ANSWERS TO: (MJ) SONG, 'THEY DON'T CARE ABOUT US!!! - 'VOTE FOR ME, AND I WILL
PROPOSE A 'LIFE SUSTAINING' AMENDMENT THAT 'WE HAVE THE RIGHT TO BEAR INTELLIGENCE IF YOU WILL;
BECAUSE IF YOU WON'T; SOCIETY IS D-O-O-M-E-D TO THIS FOREVER ON GOING STATUS QUO!!! (24)

HISTORY ON DISPLAY
RIGHTEOUSLY COMBATING MADNESS
`Vintage Journalism REVIEW & TAKEOFF POINT

When Dark Souls met God
VICTIM'S OUTRAGE (((BREAKING DOWN BARRIERS)))

WITHOUT HAVING GOD IN ONE'S LIFE; THE DEVIL WILL ARROGANTLY CLAIM YOU. THE RESULTS ARE IN! - JUST TURN ON THE TV NEWS, 'ETC, AND SEE THE MUL-TIUDINOUS NUMBER OF CRIME IMPETUOUS LOST SOUL GODLESS ZOMBIES OUT THERE THAT NEVER HAD ANY ACCESS TO THIS 'MAKE YOUR DAY' MEMO! THEREFORE, SIG-NIFICANT FAILURES OF THE STATUS QUO. WHEREBY, PROOF THEREOF, FIRST AND FOREMOST 'THE PRIORITY OF EDUCATION' IS THAT OF ONE BEING MORALLY PRI-NCIPLED, VIA ONE'S OWN PERSONAL BEHAVIOUR. ♪ I WANT YOU - TO SHOW ME THE WAY - EVERYDAY!!! INTRODUCING, FAITH BASED INITIATIVES FINEST HOUR!

`IN BRIEF: STATUS QUO, FOREVER ON GOING BULLYING, IS A DIABOLICAL BEHAVIOR, STEMMING FROM A SECULAR DOMINANTLY CONTROLLED SOCIETY!!!

♪♪ MA-MA, DON'T LET YOUR BABIES GROW-UP TO BE COW'ARDS. ♪♪

'AN EDUCATIONALLY SPEAKING EXAMPLE! "BULLIES ARE NOTHING MORE THAN 'MORALLY WEAK MINDED' INDIVIDUALS IN TAKING OUT THEIR FRUSTRATIONS ON THE OVER-ALL VULNERABLE". - WHEREAS THIS TAKES ONE OF FOREBEARING MORAL STRENGTH TO DO RIGHT; TO DO GOOD; THUS ACTIVATING THE GOLD-EN RULE' AMONG THE RIGHTEOUS... 'ONLY TRUTH CAN FREE YOU' TO GET A WORTHWHILE EDUCATION.

EDUCATIONALLY SPEAKING, WELCOME TO THE WINDUP DOLL, PLAY BY PLAY, FLESH AND BLOOD ROBOT SCHOOL OF 'POSITIVE INFLUENCE'. "INFLUENCE" IS THE RE-CALL PLUS OF ONE'S MOTIVATIONAL DECISION MAKINGS. 'THIS HERE BEING A LEGITIMATE PERMISSIBLE' STANDARDIZED EDUCATIONAL BREAKTHROUGH CHALLE-NGE ANYONE? - VIA THIS A VINTAGE TIME CAPSULE PROPOSAL!!! RENO GAZETTE JOURNAL PRINTED YOURS TRULY, BACK IN JULY 1992. WITH A LETTERS TO THE EDITOR, QUESTION RESPONSE. (QUESTION) SHOULD PRAYER BE ALLOWED AT PUBLIC SCHOOL FUNCTIONS? - ARMED WITH THE CONSTITUTION - YES. - TAKEN IN PROPER CONTEXT' TO USE THE WORD NAME GOD, AND 'ONLY THE WORD NAME GOD, WITHOUT ANY RELIGIOUS 'GENDER COERCION' IS LEAVING AN INDIVIDUAL WITH ONE'S OWN PERSONAL CONCEPT, THAT CAN BE VERY MEANINGFUL TO ONE'S DECISION MAKING IN THIS DAY AND AGE. 'A COMMON DENOMINATOR (EXAMPLE)

IN GOD WE TRUST.
PROTECT YOUR IDENTITY!
choose Halos FREE Installation...

REALITY CHECK: YOURS TRULY, A MILLION TO ONE, 20/20 PRESIDENTIAL LONG SHOT?! YET, THE WORST THING THAT COULD HAPPEN THRU ALL THIS; WOULD BE TO HAVE CHANGED THE WORLD FOR THE BETTER, THRU MY DISCOVERY..

(25)

SHOW ME — SHOW ME THE Democracy! SHOW ME THE Democracy.

Show and Tell

= BORDER CHAOS =
'IN FRONT OF THE DEVIL AND EVERYONE!!!
"HUMAN SUFFERING RULES"

Americans are fed up with Calling for Justice

'PRESIDENTAL CANDIDATES'?! — AND OR, BIPARTISANSHIPS' FINEST HOUR.
SHOULD 'YOU FIND YOURSELF SLIPPING IN THE POLLS AND WANT TO
BECOME PRAGMATICALLY, THE OMNIPOTENT 'LEAD DOG' IN THIS HERE
'OF THE PEOPLE' PRESIDENTAL CAMPAIGN; "TAKE MY ADVISE PLEASE"

'WITH THIS HERE GIFT THAT KEEPS ON GIVING'
— THUS ENDING THIS STATUS QUO NIGHTMARE! SINCERELY, L.M.T. 89503...

"My Fellow Americans ETC; Read Listen and Win!

'MAKE MEXICO OUR 51ST STATE; ALONG WITH THE REST OF THEIR GENTRIFIED
SOUTHERN NEIGHBORS TO BECOME ONE STATE. — AND YOU'LL FIND THAT 'NOBODY
WANTS TO LEAVE TOWN THERE VIA OUR, KICK BUTT A.T.F. THUS YOU'LL BE
DEALING WITH A MUCH 'KINDER AND GENT'LORE DRUG CARTELL; RIGHT
PRES.TRUMP! 'TAKEOFF POINT' KEEP THE BOARDER CLOSED FOR THE FIRST
4 YEARS SO THAT WE' CAN COME IN AND SET UP SHOP WITHOUT ANY CHAOS.
(DECLARE ENGLISH TO BE OUR OFFICIAL SPOKEN LANGUAGE) $NEED OFFICIAL
ALL NEW AMERICAN MOVE-IN CURRENCY MAKES FOR $&¢.) THUS ONCE 4 YEARS
-IN- START FREE ELECTIONS. 'A BI-LINGO WINDFALL, OVER- ALL THIS HERE
BEING A 'WIN, WIN' BETTER QUALITY OF LIFE FOR MOST PEOPLE.
— KEEP IN MIND BECAUSE OF THE WARM CLIMATIC PARADISE,
THE PAY SCALE FOR THE MOST PART WILL BE ON THE CHILLY.
(((PROPERTY SALES, AND BUSINESS EXPANSIONS GALORE;
NEW GOLF COURSES, SOCCER TO 'UM ETC!.)))

PROFESSIONAL
BASEBALL FOOTBALL BASKETBALL HOCKEY
"THE WORLD TOMORROW."

'Americanizing, We can build on one America?

` P.S. — AND TO ALL THOSE TRAVEL AGENT 'GANGS THEY GOT WORKING DOWN
THERE; WITH A LITTLE AUTHORATIVE STEADY DIET OF 'BITCH SLAPPING' THEIR
EVENTUALLY GOING TO FIND THE ELUSIVE JESUS. ☺

((BREAKING DOWN BARRIERS))) 'WELCOME TO CIVILIZATION'
— IF YOU SEE SOMETHING HERE SAY SOMETHING! (26)

" When words need to be said "
The Future of earth balance democracy is at stake.
Report places blame for Climate change global warming squarely on humans

Greenhouse gas emissions likely 'dominant cause'

(((QUESTIONING AUTHORITY)))

'SO YESTERDAY' FOR THEIR FAILURE TO RECOGNIZE THE 'EQUAL IMPACT OF -

What EVERYONE ON EARTH Needs to KNOW.

Birth control is A Realistic Survival Plan.

"OVERPOPULATION IS A MAJOR IN-GREEDY-ENT TO GLOBAL WARMING CLIMATE CHANGE"

hellish conditions. Earth in danger :
TIME SENSITIVE

- WITH ALL THE ON GOING EFFECTS OF 'GLOBAL WARMING' HAPPENING;
IT'S NOW LIKE TELLING YOUR CHILDREN; - SORRY KID'S; WE GAVE
AWAY ALL OF YOUR ENVIRONMENTAL INHERITANCE TO THE DEVIL...

time to calculate the costs?

Point-of-View *PRO-LIFE GOES INTO EFFECT THE DAY
PRO-INTELLIGENCE, (BIRTH CONTROL) COMES OF AGE.*

" CHOOSE *PRO-INTELLIGENCE."*

OF Paradise & Poverty

IRRESPONSIBILITY CULMINATES TO THIS HERE BEING A GLOBAL RESOURCE EXHAUSTING
'BABY FACTORY' POVERTY STRICKEN OVER-LOAD OF =BIBLICAL PROPORTIONS=!
-FETUS-FEED-US-FEET-US- (SHOES, etc. -FEAT-US-(JOBS, JOBS, JOBS,).
2012,"THERE'S NO SUCH THING AS OVER-
POPULATION AND PIECE ON EARTH; THE MORE THE SCARIER!" (EXAMPLE)
'ARAB SPRING' IN SYRIA, 'ETC! IN REFERENCE TO THE KILLING OF ALL
THOSE PEOPLE'-IN NOT BEING ABLE TO PROVIDE FOR THEIR WANTS AND
NEEDS, THEY ALL BECAME 'EQIVALENT' TO A HOUSE CLEANING LATE TERM
ABORTION; ALONG WITH ALL THE MULTITUDES OF TENT CITY REFUGEES,
THAT ARE ALL PRODUCTS OF 'OVERPOPULATION' THUS
AN UN-ACHIEVABLE QUALITY OF LIFE'S WORST NIGHTMARE!

SETTING THE BAR: IN RETROSPECT OF HOW 'NOT TO BECOME A CONTRIBUTING FACTOR
TO THE OVERPOPULATION, DIRT POOR POVERTY SOCIETY!? 'MASTURBATION IS THE
GRANDIS FORM OF BIRTH CONTROL' AND IN THIS HERE RELIGION, IT'S ONLY A SIN
IF YOU GET CAUGHT...

Intelligence Report story BRIEFING
ON Founder of THE POSITIVE Faith Religion,

FOR THE FIRST TIME EVER..

'FIRST' 'MAN' TO MONITOR INFLATION REPRIMANDER CZAR?!
'THERE NEEDS TO BE A CEILING PUT ON INFLATION; WATCHDOG OVERSE'ER;
THIS HERE RUNAWAY 'DOMINO EFFECT' OF GREEDY INFLATION HAS TO STOP
SOMEWHERE."WE CAN'T GO ON L-I-V-I-N-G LIKE THIS" LANDLORD ETC/
ALL THE HARD WORK THE PROTESTERS HAD PUT INTO ATTAINING A HIGHER
MINIMUM WAGE; HAS ALL BUT BEEN SCARFED UP BY THE INFLATION MONSTER!
- ALONG WITH WHAT'S BEEN 'OPEC'ING AWAY AT YOUR POCKET BOOK.
`ANOTHER EXAMPLE AS LIKE WITH 'ALL THESE PHARMACY BRO' TYPE DRUG
STORE INFLATION FREAKS; THRIVING CROSS COUNTRY THEY NEED TO BE
'ALL THROWN IN - TOUJEO...

TODAY'S MOST
WANTED ARTICLES. FACTS ON FILE Make an Impact.

"I GURU UP ON Religion AND politics."

Oper Minded Talk, "Facing Up to Reality"

'divine inspiration INVISIBLE GUIDING"

BOOK Contents

ANSWERS TO EVIDENCE OF
PERSISTENT PRAYER UNLIMITED.,

Many years, many words, from just 1 pen.,

written OPINION COMMENTARY takes time to write.,

CAPITALIZE ON Time Well Spent Serving Your Needs.

Powerful Testimony

The Wait Is Over.

MAXIMUM EXPOSURE PREVENTION

That was then...

♫ *"It's The End Of The World As We Know It"*

'revolution'.
ENOUGH IS ENOUGH!

"Great lessons in protests"

"OVER-ALL, MENTAL HEALTH CARES FINEST HOUR"

Defining mission a must read.

"PATRIOTISM IS THE BACKBONE OF OUR COUNTRY'
YOURS TRULY, BEST RESTORER OF"

Celebrate America

AMERICAN WRITERS INSTITUTE PROUDLY PRESENTS

JOURNALIST RELEASE OF <u>NEW BOOK ENTITLED</u>

The
C H R O N I C L E S
of
Dr. Sunday

"Presenting GOD'S INSPIRED WORD!"

WANTED

New leader, new nation, new world

'READ <u>HIM</u> AND WEEP'

"My Fellow Americans" **FRIAR FLYER** Discovery Kit

((ANSWERS TO MYSTERIOUS END OF AN AGE PROPHECY FULFILLED))

(((BOOK EXCERPT))) THE P-O-R-P-O-I-S-E OF LIFE —
IS TO SERVE GOD, THRU "HUMAN-KIND" AND `NOT TO BECOME
SHELL-FISH • FACTORY REBORN; I'LL S-E-A YOU AT THE BOOK SIGNING.

= OR = *The `Real Day The Earth Stood Still* (29)

'MARTIAN PEEPHOLE' DITCH JUNEAU RAT NOW BAYPEE, OLIVE IN WE KNOW, ENVY

Writer's on the storm !

"PEOPLE SHOULD 'NOT BE DISCRIMINATED AGAINST."

AN AFTER SCHOOL SPECIAL MADE TO ORDER.

"THE TIME IS HERE. THE TIME IS NOW. THIS IS THE MOMENT."

'THESIS-CHRIST PEOPLE' IN TESTIMONY WHEREOF

'TELL IT LIKE IT IS' **Biblical Correctness**

Does God have a sexual gender?

#METOO **Life Lessons as Timeless as Infinity**

'ALWAYS WAS AND ALWAYS WILL BE' GOD Holy Spirit' (EOE) IS THE POSITIVE SPIRIT = <u>WITHOUT GENDER</u>.

"TRUTH IS STRANGER THAN FICTION"

(SCRIPTURE'S FINEST HOUR)

' MISOGYNIST PARLOR, **STORYBOOK ON** THE ORIGINAL SIN;

PROMOTION OF TOP BILLING 'GENDER' MAN-IPULATION.

'GLOBALLY SPEAKING; HISTORICALLY, 'FOR THE MOST PART WOMEN'
HAVE BEEN BACK SEAT JERKED AROUND FOR ATLEAST A COUPLE OF WEEKS NOW!!!

And best Quote award goes to

"HISTORY, HAS ALWAYS BEEN - HIS - STORY".

$$$ 'WAR OF THE COLD SHOULDER!

"FEATURING STATIONS OF THE DOUBLE CROSSED"

'SO MANY WOMEN TO RELIGIOUSLY EMANCIPATE; 'SO LITTLE TIME!!!

☞ (2018) "THE POPE STATES TO A GAY MAN, THAT GOD LOVES HIM".
(COMMENT) 'A DAY LATE, AND MULTITUDES OF SUICIDE VICTIMS SHORT...
"FOR WHAT STARTED WITH 'RELIGION, CAN ONLY BE 'RECTIFIED BY RELIGION!"
"I'M NOT BRAGGING, I'M COMPLAINING!!!
THE 'LGBT' WRITTEN IN STONE 'NEW-AGE' BIBLICAL
REFORMATION; NON-DISCRIMINATORY, CAKE POWER TURNAROUND
ACCEPTANCE BIBLE; HAPPENS THRU ME; OR THIS 'NEVER' HAPPENS"...
'THEREFORE, THE PURCHASE OF THIS BOOK ON A GRAND SCALE SHOWS
JUSTICE WILL PREVAIL'!! - GOD LOVE YA - WELCOME TO THE POSITIVE
FAITH, 'ONE WORLD RELIGION' CONVERSION KIT. - RIGHT ORLANDO?!
IN REFERENCE TO 'LGBT' DISCRIMINATORY PRACTICES.
THE INCUMBENT NEANDERTHAL RELIGION; 'DEUTERONOMY' IS NOW

-DUDE-WILL-RAT-ON-ME!

FAITH FORUM

Religion classes in public schools?

Yes !!! "People should not be discriminated against."

THE PRIORITY OF EDUCATION IS THAT OF BEING A 'MORAL ONE. <u>ETC</u>. ETC. (30)

'MAKING THE WORLD A BETTER PLACE TO LIVE 'HOW TO GUIDE'

An expert's prayer

GOT GOD?

US 'VERSUS' THEM.

- BREAK ON THRU TO THE
'POSITIVE' SIDE!!!

"People should not be discriminated against."

'WELCOME TO THE MIRACLE OF UNDERSTANDING'

"ONLY TRUTH CAN FREE YOU"

GO DEEP!!!

☞ BLESSED ARE THE "TRUE" LOVERS OF GOD; FOR WITHIN THIS
LIVE WIRE, INTERACTIVE PRAYER RAPPORT WITH GOD;
RACISM DOESN'T EXIST!!!

"WHEREAS, WE'RE ALL ONE IN THE SAME PEOPLE, RESPONSIBLE
FOR THE SAFETY AND WELL-BEING OF ALL PEOPLE".
'PEOPLE COME IN ALL KIND OF 'COLORS, SHAPES,
AND SIZES; BE NICE TO THEM 'ALL./'ONE MIND FITS 'ALL.

AMEN...

(While You Were Out MESSAGE EXTENSION)

'PRAYER CONTEXT REALITY CHECK √
- UPON FURTHER REVIEW -

#1. THIS HERE BEING A 'NEW-AGE VALIDITY' AND ACCEPTANCE POLICY,
TOWARDS 'ALL RELIGIONS!!!

#2. CREATS A CONSCIOUSNESS TO THE PLIGHT OF ALL THE POVERTY
STRICKEN 'HAVE NOTS...

#3. POINT-BLANK, BULLY PREVENTION AWARENESS...

#4. COMFORTING PRAYER 'IS A FULFILLING CURE FOR LONELINESS
AND INSECURITY; THUS A FORMULA TO ONE'S LOVING ONESELF,
- AND OR, IN ORDERING A PIZZA. ·‿·

IN CONCLUSION: END OF DAZE ON BORROWED TIME;
- SHOWSTOPPER - SIGNED: DR. SUNDAY
= 'NOBEL PEACE PRIZE WINNING - LARRY IT - ANYONE???

🎼 Give'em some of that new-time religion
...And They Lived Happily Ever After."

(31)

In Good Company

'Where Everybody Knows Your Name'

Your Guide To Tha Best Local Bars And Clubs Begins With A Solving Tha Crisis

Happy Hour

PAGE

"It's All Good"

APPEARING NIGHTLY

FREE

Speech, **rescue**

mission THA First

Amendment."

"SOME OF THA PLACES I'VE BARTENDED AT; A PABST SMEAR IS WHEN A WOMAN SLOPPILY GUZZLES DOWN A BLUE RIBBON BEER, THEN WIPES HER CHIN OFF WITH HER FOREARM."

YOUR A CAB!

JESUS — CAME INTO MY BAR THA OTHER DAY., I DIDN'T SERVE HIM CAUSE HE LOOKED LIKE HE, WAS ALREADY HAMMERED!

IN A CIRCULAR BAR ONCE THA BALL GAME IS OVER AND THA TRUTH SERUM KICKS IN., POLITICS AND RELIGION, SEEM TO BECOME MY CUSTOMERS MAIN TOPICS OF CONVERSATION.

IT COMES IN A GLASS!

The opposition is in session

free from gender bias, *Someone must stand up to*

"WHAT STARTED WITH RELIGION CAN ONLY BE RECTIFIED BY RELIGION". **(YEAH, RIGHT)** *Humans need to evolve.*

'SPIRITUALLY'

#WeSeeEqual SPOKEN HERE. (32)

What's the coolest story from scripture?

JESUS, AT 'THE LAST SUPPER' AFTER DRINKING HIS FILL OF MAD DOG 20/20 WINE,
OR ENOUGH TO GET A OVER TWICE THE ALCOHOL LIMIT DONKEY DRIVING D.U.I. STATES
TO HIS APOSTLES. (JESUS) MIRACLES!!?? IF WALKING ON -ICE- OR A WATER
WASN'T GOOD ENOUGH FOR THE ROMANS TO MAKE THEM A BELIEVER OF ME;
"WAIT TILL I SHOW THEM HOW I CAN WALK ALL OVER BUREAUCRATIC GRID'LOCK;
THAT'S THE MIRACLE I'M TALKING ABOUT!" THE LEAST POLITICAL WORD EVER
USED IN WASHINGTON IS CALLED BIPARTISANSHIP; AND I PLAN ON CHANGING THAT
BY INVENTING TOP 'ROMAN NOODLES!'IN TWO YEARS I'LL BE OLD ENOUGH TO RUN FOR
PRESIDENT AND I'M GOING TO PICK THAT ASS-WHOLE * KANYE, TO BE MY VICE-
PRESIDENT; JUST TO PROVE THAT EVERYONE WILL STILL VOTE FOR ME...
          - PRIOR TO BEING APPREHENDED BY THE AUTHORTIES, AS THE STORY GOES-
THAT'S WHEN JESUS PLOTED TO OVER'THROW THE ROMAN GOVERNMENT IN NEED OF HELP-
ING THE POOR, BY WAY OF TELLING PONTIUS PILOT, THAT 'HE WAS GOD IN THE FLESH'
- AND PILOT'S RESPONSE TO HIM WAS - YOU GUYS ARE A DIME A DOZEN; 'YOU, JIM
JONES, DAVID KORESH, CHARLES MAN-SON! - AND JESUS RESPONDS - BUT WAIT A MIN-
UTE , I'M THE MESSIAH; AND PILOT SAID PROVE IT?! 'JESUS THEN RESPONDS 'HE
WHO IS WITHOUT SIN, CAST THE FIRST NECULAR WARHEAD!!! - FEELING INTIMATED,
AND IGNORANT TO THE SITUATIONAL UP-GRADE, PILOT SAYS - CRUCIFY HIM - ...
- JUST DOWN THE STREET WHERE JUDAS WHO DIDN'T BUY INTO THE STORY; THUS RE-
CEIVED MONEY FOR RATTING ON JESUS; THEN OUT OF HIS GUILT TOOK THAT MONEY AND
BET IT ALL ON THE GONZAGA JESUITS, IN HONOR OF JESUS, TO WIN THE 2017, COLL-
EGE BASKETBALL NATIONAL CHAMPIONSHIP GAME - AND FINAL SCORE, HANGED HIMSELF.
- IN THIS HERE DEVELOPING STORY; MARY MAGDALENE, IN SEARCH OF FINDING JESUS,
FINALLY FINDS HIM AT THE CROSS. MARY SPEAKING, 'THE PEOPLE WERE ALL TELLING
ME THAT THEY SAW YOU, AND THAT YOU GOT HAMMERED; I THOUGHT THAT THEY WERE ALL
TALKING ABOUT AT THE 'LAST SUPPER' WHERE YOU TURNED WINE INTO WATER! - SO WHAT
DID YOU DO TO DESERVE ALL THIS? - AND JESUS RESPONDS, HONEY 'I SHRUNK' THE
KIDS! - "ALL GOD'S CHILDREN"... - MEAN WHILE, ON THE OTHER SIDE OF TOWN
WHERE APOSTLE PETER, THE FIRST POPE 'WHO WAS A <u>FISHERMAN</u> WITH NO SHORTAGES
OF TELLING <u>WHOPPERS</u> WAS SELLING HIS STORY OF ADVANTAGES TO THE ONE % ERS!
'PETER SPEAKING, THIS WAY THERE'S ONLY 'ONE UNIQUE 'SON OF GOD' HERO HERE,
THAT'S JESUS! - AND 'ALL YOU GUYS GET TO HERD YOUR WEALTH WITHOUT ANY GUILT.
OR BACK'LASH; THUS LEAVING THE REST OF SOCIETY OUT THERE IN BEING CONSIDERED
          AS NOTHING MORE THAN A BUNCH OF <u>BARGAINLESS</u>

'Nobodies.'

I'LL EVEN TOSS IN 'HE DIED FOR YOUR SIN' IT'S IMPRESSIVE TO ALL THE SIMPLE
MINDED PEOPLE OUT THERE! - ONE % ERS RESPONDING, AND WE'LL MAKE SURE THAT
          YOUR ORGANIZATION 'NEVER HAS TO PAY ANY TAXES! ☺ DEAL ...
     IN CONCLUSION: THE GENESIS OF REAL NEWS (VS) FAKE —YOU BE THE JUDGE;
'closing into the gap between rich & poor; thus creation of a conscious'!!!

AUTHOR'S NOTE: - AS A YOUTH GROWING UP I, WAS SENTENCED TO DOING A 8, YEAR
STINT IN A PAROCHICAL SCHOOL; I PAID MY DEBT TO SOCIETY; WHEREAS THIS IS
WHERE ALL THIS THOUGHT PROVOKING INFORMATION DERIVED FROM...
*
NAME CALLING, WORTHY FROM THE TAYLOR SWIFT PARALLAX ORDEAL,THAT TOOK PLACE ETC.
     THE REASON YOU NEVER HEARD THAT MUCH IN THE BIBLE
       ABOUT JOSEPH THE FATHER OF JESUS, IS THAT WHEN HE AND MOTHER
   MARY WENT TO DIVORCE COURT; HE TOLD THE JUDGE THAT 'JESUS WAS BORN
    OF A VIRGIN' SO THAT HE COULD GET OUT OF PAYING ANY KIND OF CHILD
SUPPORT; HE AUTUALLY WAS THE FIRST ONE WHO COIN PHRASED THE STATEMENT
   'I DID NOT HAVE SEX WITH THAT WOMAN' AND THE REST IS BIBLICAL HISTORY.(33)

WHO'S THE BEST 'REANIMATE SALES PERSON,
TEACHER SPOKESPERSON, FOR GOD?
'YOURS TRULY, AT YOUR
SERVICE!

'IN BRIEF
EXAMPLE' 'RELIGIOUSLY SPEAKING, WHAT WE HAVE HERE IS A HISTORIC
FAILURE TO RATIONALIZE. THEREFORE, A 'RE-REASONING RELOAD,
STARTING WITH THE FIRST AND FOREMOST COMMANDMENT! "I AM 'THE
LORD THY GOD, THOU SHELT 'NOT HAVE 'ANY FALSE 'gods'BEFORE ME".
OR 'CLOSE ENOUGH FOR RELIGIOUS WORK'. 'INTELLECTUALLY SPEAKING,
'HISTORICALLY SPEAKING, "NOBODY ABSORBED THE MEMO"...

(REVISITED EXAMPLES.) HISTORY 1927, START OF WORK ON THE DON'T
TRY TO CON---GOD THE POSITIVE SPIRIT, = ABOUT YOUR FALSE god CREATION
CELEBRATION OF MT. RUSHMORE, THUS GOLDEN FLEECE, INTHAT SAY CHEESE 'GOD
ONLY PICTURED US HERE! RESULTING IN THE 1929 STOCK MARKET CRASH, ALONG WITH
30'S DUST BOWL AND DEPRESSION; LEADING ALL THE WAY UP TO THE 1941, COMPLETION
OF MT. RUSHMORE, AND THE WELCOMING INTO WWII, OR 'HELL ON EARTH PERSONIFIED.
UPGRADED FROM THE REST OF US SLOBS, PRIOR TO THE HOLOCAST; THE JEWISH PEOPLE
WERE ONCE REFERRED TO AS THE CHOSEN PEOPLE; AND DEMON POSSESSED HITLER,
ACCOMMODATED. RECONFIRMING ALL GOD'S CHILDREN. August 2005 *HURRICANE KATRINA
CREATIVE CURRENTS! BLAME IT ON THE 'RIO FALSE GOD SON WORLD, WORSHIP EXHIBIT.*

'GOLDEN FLEECE REVISITED,
REFLECTIVELY, HOW ABOUT THE EASTER ISLAND 'FALSE GOD,
STATUE CREATION STORY, OF ALL THOSE PEOPLE THAT VANISHED ●

What you need to know

YOU CAN'T TOSS 'THE' BOSS FOR A LOSS.
'ONLY GOODNESS COMES FROM GOD'.
"GOD, HOLY SPIRIT IS A CONSTANT; PURE LOVE'S ONE AND ONLY
SENDER, 'THE POSITIVE SPIRIT WITHOUT GENDER. IN ACCORDANCE
WITH - TO LITERALLY PUSH GOD'S SPIRITUAL MESSAGE AWAY! - AN
EVIL LURKING godZILLA, FILLING IN THE GAP WILL ALWAYS BE THERE
TO ACCOMODATE YOU. **WAKE UP AND SMELL THE BARRAGE OF ON GOING DEMONIC
DISASTERS THAT HAVE BEEN TAKING PLACE!** A ATMOSPHERIC WEATHER PREVAILING
DEVASTATION ●

INVESTIGATING THE ON GOING SPIRITUAL BATTLE GAME
OF POSITIVE 'RAIN, (**versus**) NEGATIVE 'RAIN, EXAMPLE ETC.
ELEMENTS OF POSITIVITY VS. ELEMENTS OF NEGATIVITY! NEGATIVE COMPONENTS
OF HIGH WINDS, DRY CONDITIONS CONDUCIVE TO ALL THOSE CALIFORNIA FIRES...
ATMOSPHERIC POSITIVE SPIRIT. ((VERSUS)) ATMOSPHERIC NEGATIVE SPIRIT

'Life' *according to* A LARGE SCALE WEATHER PREVAILING ENVIRONMENT.   ARMAGEDDON
TO YOU YET!?

THE SEARCH FOR SIGNS OF INTELLIGENT LIFE IN THE UNIVERSE?

"WELCOME TO THE ROCKET SCIENCE GRADUATE SCHOOL OF READING AND
COMPREHENSION! YOURS TRULY, THE ROCKET SCIENTOLOGIST THAT'S
GONE FATHER, OR A' FURTHER, THAN ANY FLESH AND BLOOD MAN".

FRIAR FLYER NEWSLETTERCOMMENTARY
'BY THE NEW WORLD ADAM'

JUNE/JULY
2018

FEATURING: "Storytelling on a grand scale"
Laying Claim to Ministry of Higher Education ...

(((TWEET OF THE MONTH)))

T V, TELL ALL BIPARTISAN MUDSLINGING (VS) YOURS TRULY, MAGNUMOPUS!
- MAKING THE <u>WORDS</u> A BETTER PLACE TO LIVE?! 'BE PERCEPTIVE WITH THE
POSITIVE; PROCRASTINATE THE NEGATIVE; "TO SPEAK KIND WORDS IS TO
HEAR KIND ECHOES" - THUS WELCOME TO CIVILIZATION...

SURMOUNTABLE 'FAKE NEWS' STARTED BACK
IN THE LIFE AND TIMES OF JESUS;

THE ADVENTURE BEGINS HERE.

FROM STONE-AGE BAPTISM, TO MODERN-DAY BRAIN WASHING! IN TURNING THE
AGE OF REASON AS A YOUNG OPEN MINDED CATHOLIC SCHOOL CHILD; I WAS
TAUGHT THAT JESUS, LITERALLY <u>TURNED STONE INTO BREAD</u>! 'UPDATE UPSTAGE
REALITY CHECK' (VS) YOURS TRULY! 'IF I CAN <u>TURN</u> A BUS LOAD OF <u>STONE</u>
FACED 1%ERS FACES <u>INTO</u> A SMILE; THENCE BE PLENTY ENOUGH <u>BREAD</u> TO GO
AROUND FOR EVERYBODY!!!

HISTORICALLY SPEAKING, BACKED BY THE 'WHO'S ZOOMING WHO BELIEF
SYSTEM OF THE DEVOTE CLERGY, 'PEDOPHILE ASSOCIATION,
THUS MAKING THEM FEEL COMFORTABLE WITHIN THEIR OWN BEHAVIOR...
"SOME OF THE PEOPLE SOME OF THE TIME, MOST OF THE PEOPLE MOST OF THE TIME, ETC")

THE "MAJOR LEAGUE" 'MIRACLE OF CONVINCABLE ACHIEVEMENT' WOULD HAVE BEEN;
'IF HE COULD HAVE WALKED ALL-OVER BUREAUCRATIC GRIDLOCK! - HE COULD HAVE
LEARNED ALOT FROM 'FAKE NEWS' TRUMP; ALONG WITH HAVING CREDENCE FOR MY'

(PARALLEL PHENOMENON CONTINUED) 'NOT TO BE DENIED! I CAUGHT 3 FISH,
IN THE GLOW WITH THE FLOW FUKUSHIMA RUN OFF; SO I ENVITED OVER 300,
PEOPLE TO MY PLACE TO EAT DINNER; AND WHEN I TOLD EVERYBODY WHERE
I CAUGHT THE FISH AT!!! 'EVERYBODY TOLD ME THAT THEY HAD ALREADY EATEN...

- AND AS THIS REVOLUTIONARY PREACHER WILL TELL YOU; RUMOR ALREADY HAS
IT THAT <u>I</u> WAS DELIVERED BY A STORK...

- WITH ALL THESE 'DEVIL CONTROLLED' NATIONWIDE 'HELL FIRES' TAKING
PLACE OUT THERE; IT'S KIND OF LIKE A WELCOME TO A VISUAL LIVING
'END OF DAZE ON BORROWED TIME' IN SEARCH OF A 'YOURS TRULY SAVIOR'
OUT OF THE 'BULL' PEN; THUS BOOK FORTIFIED 'YOUR WINNING LOTTERY
TICKET OUT OF HELL-SINKI GUIDE...

READINGS FOR REASONING

<u>1982,</u> 'MY RESPONSE TO SHAKESPEARE. YES! "THE WORLD IS A STAGE" - AND OR,
IN MY WORDS LIFE IS NOTHING BUT A 'PLAY' ON WORDS, OR A WORLDS! IT'S ALL
KIND OF LIKE ONE BIG REAL LIFE PERSONAL MOVIE GOING ON OUT THERE; AND I
HAVE TO ADMIT FROM TIME TO TIME - I SLEPT THRU IT. :"

 learning from tha past. a study in history. (35)

This Week's Biggest Release

Secrets From Tha History of an Old Idea

Tha Making of 'HIStory'

= SOME 40 YEARS, AFTER = AND THE REASON FOR CHURCH PAYING NO TAXES =

Class 101: Global Mythmaking is motivated entirely by greed=

AND OR, THA HOODWINKING 'ONE PERCENT' ETC, TICKET HOLDERS 'UNCONTESTED REASON FOR BEING. (VS) YOURS TRULY, THA PROPHET THAT BELIEVES IN PROFIT SHARING; INOVATOR CAPITALIST THAT BELIEVES WE CAN 'ALL CAPITALIZE TOGETHER!!!

written 1983

THA GOVERNMENT AND IT'S MEDIA

BELIEVES THAT JESUS CHRIST IS GOD, AS MUCH AS A HERION ADDICT BELIEVES IN SANTA CLAUS!

But

AS LONG AS THEY CAN KEEP YOU SWEET-N-LOW THAT SOME MAN IS OR WAS FAR MORE HONORABLE THAN YOURSELF: TO ALL OPPRESSED PEOPLE / A PENNY FOR YOUR THOUGHTS.

Advocate for homeless ETC :

Sidewalk-Speaker, City of Reno

LICENSE #: 126200

EXPIRATION DATE:

CLOCK IS TICKING ON

♫ IN THE YEAR <u>2025</u>,

IF MAN IS STILL ALIVE ???

BIGGEST LITTLE CITY IN THE WORLD

CITY OF RENO®

The ERADICATION
OF HUMAN MISERY
PROJECT.

WITH *The Gospel according to*
"ALL GOD'S CHILDREN, HISTORIC
INAUGURAL DECLARATION".

The art of restoring magnetic heads.

☞ "**GREATEST BOOK EVER WRITTEN**".

Scripture **THE WILL**. WHERE THERE'S A 'W-I-L-L' THERE'S A WAY!!!
'GOD FRENDED ME' TO VOUCH-SAFE 'ALL THE POVERTY STRICKEN NEEDY WITH
'<u>THE NECESSITIES OF LIFE</u>'; VIA THRU THE 'GLOBAL' GENEROSITY OF
'ALL THE MULTI-BILLIONAIRES; MULTI-MILLIONAIRES;
THAT CARE TO BE RECOGNIZED BEFORE GOD, AND THE WHOLE WORLD
IN THIS HERE UP-MOST PRESTEGOUS BOOK;
BY WAY OF DONATING 'HALF OF ONE'S WEALTH; YOU'LL BE
'BIBLICALLY HONORED AND REMEMBERED TILL THE END OF TIME...
STORY BOOK SIGNED BY: THE QUINTESSENTIAL ROBIN HOOD.

Time to Rescue THE NEANDERTHAL DISCRIMINATORY *Once Upon A Time* **Bible'** ETC, ETC.
REWRITTEN FOR THE PEOPLE OF OUR TIMES, AND 'ALL TIMES'... (37)

WINNING A WAR OF WORDS
(Closing tha Case on <u>GREED</u>) Page
Survival A big motivating factor
Report from tha Front

NATIONAL AFFAIRS
GAP victims get their day in court .

(1983)
To tha rescue
THE LAW

The Positive SPIRIT, long reach:

did you know THA SPECIFIC DEFINITION OF <u>GREED</u> IS ANY PERSON <u>HAVING OR WANTING MORE THAN</u> WITHIN A LIFE TIME, THA 'REALISTIC <u>NECESSITYS OF</u> "<u>CHOICE</u>" IN FOOD, CLOTHING, SHELTER, TRANSPORTATION, NEEDLESS TO SAY MEDICAL ATTENTION, IN THAT MAN'S PLIGHT ALONE IN LIFE IS ATLEAST WORTHY ENOUGH TO COVER ALL THA MINIMAL!

Nobody beats him in blame game ...

"unforgettable images"
'Exorcism' is fascinating !

QUESTION: WHAT'S 'YOUR RELIGIOUS DEPOSITION IN REGARDS TO EXORCISM? "WE SPECIALIZE IN USING A HAND HELD 'DIRT DEVIL' VACUUM CLEANER TO SUCK THE DEVIL RIGHT OUT OF THE OMINOUS; ALONG WITH THE 'INXS' SONG PLAYING IN THE BACKGROUND = ♫ EVERYONE THE DEVIL INSIDE! 'PROCEDURE ENDURES TILL THE ONE THAT'S IN A PREDOMINATE DEMONIAC TRANCE' UTTERS THE TRANS-ITIONAL WORD 'CHIQUITO'! THEREFORE, REGENERATING ONE BACK TO NORMALITY... ☺

GOSPEL FICTIONS
REFORM TAKES SHAPE
A Straight Look at Questions That Linger,
Biblical Correctness, 'Let's Leave tha Ice Age' **'tell it like it is'**

ON #666? BIBLICAL PSYCHO BABBLING bad news Hype Scare

PROGRA*BOGUS*MING **replaced by** A WHOLE NEW MEANING!

♩ ((INSX-MANIFEST-SONG)) 'EVERYONE THA DEVIL ♩

INSIDE!!!
MYTH vs. REALITY
FOR THA RECORD

I'M ABOUT AS THREATENING AS A DEVILED EGG.

♫ HEAVEN'S BELLS! IF YOU'RE 'EVIL YOU'RE - 'NO'- FRIEND OF MINE.
ETC!

A WAKE- UP CALL EXHIBIT Message is Forever.

RAJAN ZED **FAITH FORUM** RENO GAZETTE-JOURNAL/RGJ.COM

What is tha worst evil out there?
= WHAT EVER 'SINKS' YOUR BOAT!!! =

1. WAR: 'SPIT ON THEIR GRAVE' TERRORIST, MASSMURDERER, SERIAL KILLER.
LIFE TAKING FIRES' TSUNAMI, HURRICANE, DEVASTATING TORNADO, FLOODING.

((GREED IS NOT GOOD.))

coronavirus
(((P-A-N-D-E-M-I-C)))
When words need to be said.

Time Out! AUTHOR'S NOTE: FROM TIME, TO TIME, ALL THROUGHOUT THIS
HERE BOOK; YOU'LL BE RUNNING INTO SOME STATEMENTS BEING
REPEATED; - JUST LOOK AT THEM AS JUST BEING A REMINDER!!!
THANK YOU...

Extra, extra! Reality Check BIG GOTCHA!!!

WITH ALL THOSE 'NEAR DEATH EXPERIENCE' CONFESSORS OUT THERE; REMINISCING ON HOW
THEY VIRTUALLY SAT ON JESUS' LAP AND ATE PANCAKES --- AFTER ALL THESE YEARS WHY
HASN'T THERE 'EVER BEEN ANYONE OUT THERE PROCLAIMING THAT THEY WERE PAINFULLY'
DANCING WITH THA DEVIL ON RED HOT COALS IN PITHFORK CITY??? DON'T LOOK AT ME!
- THIS IS 'NOT A TESTIMONIAL. ☺

(39)

Democracy

page (40)

Tha Buck Starts Here.

♪ RETROSPECTIVELY EVERYBODY WANTS TO RULE ♫
♪ THA WORLD. WHEREBY EVERYBODY SHOULD
VIA THE POSITIVE, INSTRUMENTING THA
REALITY OF GOD'S WORLD...

GOD
(WORKING THROUGH MAN)

SOUL IS THE AURA OF ONE'S INNER GOODNESS.
FOR ONLY TRUE LEADERSHIP WOULD ACCEPT
POSITIVE INPUT; THUS DEMOCRACY'S FINENESS HOUR.

writer's
MARCH 3, 1995 **POINT OF VIEW** on Social Security

KEEP IT SOLVENT FOREVER, TRUST ME!

ANYTHING LESS WOULD BE UNCIVILIZED.

"LIFE IS LIKE A BOX OF CHOCOLATE COVERED TURTLES,
IN THIS CASE YOU KNOW WHAT YOUR GOING TO GET."

seeing our way clear

ON WITH THE SHOW

Connecting with humanity yet

Unfortunately, tha world doesn't know it. !

Writer traces roots of religion

"FOR WHAT STARTED WITH 'RELIGION; CAN ONLY BE 'RECTIFIED BY RELIGION!!!"

"IN BRIEF: *Life according to* **a new modern DAY** <u>RELIGIOUS</u> **CLEAN SLATE."**

exemplifies What you needed to know **AND** Process.

Life Lessons as Timeless as Infinity

"Storytelling on a grand scale"

THE POSITIVE Faith Religion

Laying Claim to Ministry of Higher Education ...

A UNIQUE SOURCE **of** SUPERIOR WISDOM

Religious Science training program

New Age **Make a difference** Bible School

THE ONE and only GOD

PERFORMS <u>MIRACLES.</u> 'NOT' STRUCTTLED MAN., BUT THROUGH MAN BY <u>GOD.</u> NOW THAT'S THE **POSITIVE** SPIRIT.

--EXAMPLE

THA MIRACLE OF MODERN DAY MEDICINE, AVIATION, 'UNDER- STANDING' -ETC-ETC-ETC-ETC-ETC- GOD <u>WORKING THRU MAN.</u>

DR. SUNDAY 'Story 1985 VS.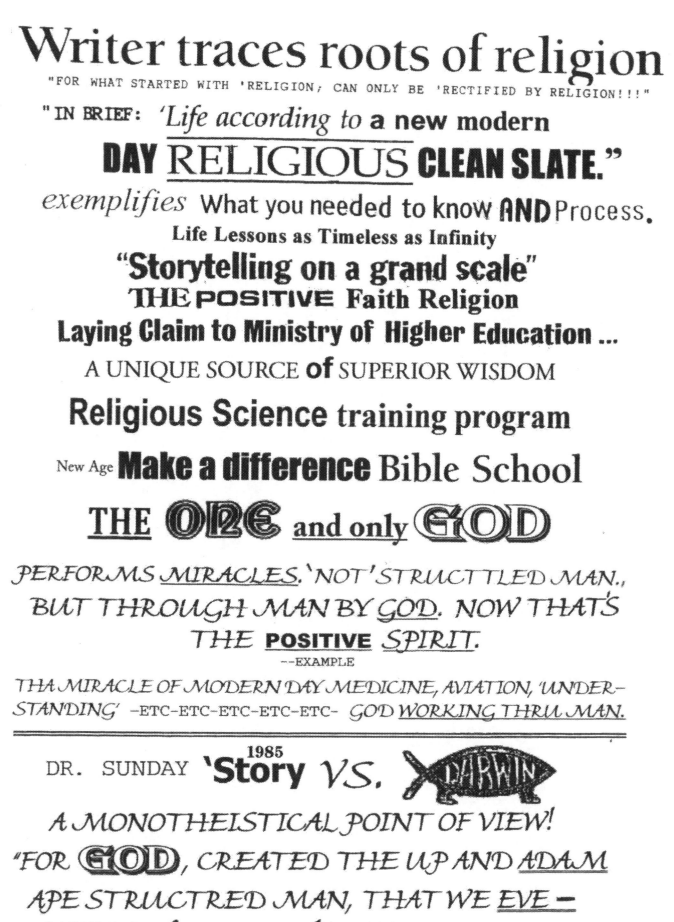

A MONOTHEISTICAL POINT OF VIEW!

"FOR GOD, CREATED THE UP AND <u>ADAM</u> APE STRUCTRED MAN, THAT WE <u>EVE</u> – VOLVED from **controversy."**

What to do when your beliefs are challenged?

'Children of a Lesser Image *of* God HOSTAGES (VS) YOURS TRULY.

DEAR God, I'M SORRY I, HAD TO PUT THA BITE ON THOSE CHRISTIANS; BUT THEY RATTLED THIS

 Lions CAGE.

"Go ahead. Ask me something and see if I'm not as wise as some silly man in a loincloth.

COURAGEOUS Lion PUBLIC — FOR — UM •

'WELL, THEY GAMBLED WITHIN MY MIND'S TEMPLE OF TRUTH; SO I SHOWED THEM MY VOCIFERATE (SAMSON WITHOUT VIOLENCE ACADEMY AWARD ROUTINE.) FOR THEY HAD ALL THEIR CHRISTIAN PARAPHER ~ NAIL YA EXCUSES IN ORDER; HIGHLIGHTED BY he DIED FOR OUR SIN'S. IT SOUNDED MORE LIKE THEY NEEDED THAT IRRESPONSIBLE POSITION TO CON·STITUTE THEIR LIBERTIES TO A DISRESPECTFUL LIFE STYLE. •

. . . .

'THE SPAGHETTISBERG ADDRESS' : FEBRUARY 14th, 2011

THIS HERE BEING THE "VERBAL, AND OR LITERARY" SAINT VALENTINE'S DAY MASSACRE. 'THIS COMPUTER IS MY SWORD BECAUSE THERE'S ONLY ONE LORD, AND MASTER... RELIGIOUSLY SPEAKING, I KNOW EVERYBODY'S LOOKING FOR RIG---ATONI! - BUT I'M THE REAL ANGEL HAIR, ▬▬ MANICOTTI THAT YOU NEED TO BE DEALING WITH. PERSONALLY I'M FETACHINI UP WITH ALL THOSE PHONY DEMOCRACY PREACHING IM-PASTA-S ANTI-PASTA, CONDEMN'ERS; SOMEDAY THEIR ALL GOING TO REGETA ALL THIS ▬ORZO THEY SAY! 'SO ALL I'M ASKING YOU TO DO IS TO USE YOUR NOODLE AND ROTELLE ON THE ONE'S THAT ARE STELLINE DEMOCRACY FROM YOU! *Politicians love to have Neanderthal religion shoved down the throats of common folk people in hopes that they'll all behave themselves; in that common folk people would love to have Neanderthal religion shoved down the throats of politicians in hopes of obtaining better policies!!!*
Obviously everybody knew I'd speak a strange language, being a gentile "natured" revolutionary Robot; and are they in for a surprise when they examine me, and find out that my dandruff isn't really computer chips after all; for sure by then my name will 'also become a universal 'cuss word, (Parallels anyone!). SIGNED: A.K.A.

EXPERIENCE
'HAVING A BEAUTIFUL MIND'
(SERMON)

Church of Open Door **MINISTER's** (Message is Forever.) challenge is teaching TOMORROW IN *Education TODAY.* **Religious** Science training program

= HIGHWAY TO HEAVEN ON 'EARTH' =

programing

takes center stage
According to
personal
RESPONSIBILITY !

<u>CREDIBILITY</u>

ANYONE ?"

THEREFORE THIS HERE BEING A 'RECREATING YOURSELF' HOW TO GUIDE
IN ACCORDANCE WITH/ ACADEMY AWARDS PROGRAMING TESTIMONY TO GOOD LIVING
IN A PERFORMANCE ARTIST! LOSING THEIR RELIGION AND GAINING "HOW I
GOT RELIGION ACTORS"! THIS DOESN'T TAKE A GENIUS TO FIGURE OUT
THE RISE OF THIS STAR REFORMER. (((ENROLLMENT))) ANYONE?
COMMON KNOWLEDGE IS TO KNOW GOD LOVES YOU, AND THAT GOD IS FORGIVING;
INTHAT TO CLAIM THE REALITY OF MORAL RELIGIOUS CONVICTION,
IS IN ALWAYS BEING WORTHY OF GOD'S LOVE.
ACTIVATING SCRIPT LIGATURE! LIGHTS, CAMERA, SOUL MISSION - BORN - AGAIN.
"WRITTEN BY YOURS TRULY" A FORMER EMPLOYEE OF THE MONTH AT DIAL A PRAYER.
`ESSAY IN CONCLUSION 'MY WORK IS DONE HERE'...

(43)

'THIS THING IS NOT OVER'.

"IN BRIEF: *Life according to* **a new modern**

DAY RELIGIOUS CLEAN SLATE."

AN AFTER SCHOOL SPECIAL MADE TO ORDER.

NO EXPIRATION DATE, PEDOPHILIA PLAYGROUND ETC;

CHURCH EXPRESSES FEAR OF GOD

'TELL IT LIKE IT IS'

'ONLY GOODNESS COMES FROM GOD'.

"GOD, HOLY SPIRIT IS A CONSTANT; PURE LOVE'S ONE AND ONLY
SENDER, 'THE POSITIVE SPIRIT WITHOUT GENDER. IN ACCORDANCE
WITH - TO LITERALLY PUSH GOD'S SPIRITUAL MESSAGE AWAY! - AN
EVIL LURKING godZILLA, FILLING IN THE GAP WILL ALWAYS BE THERE
TO ACCOMODATE YOU. **WAKE UP AND SMELL THE BARRAGE OF ON GOING DEMONIC
DISASTERS THAT HAVE BEEN TAKING PLACE!** An exclusive book excerpt.
INVESTIGATING THE ON GOING SPIRITUAL BATTLE GAME /
ATMOSPHERIC POSITIVE SPIRIT. ((VERSUS)) ATMOSPHERIC NEGATIVE SPIRIT

'THESIS-CHRIST PEOPLE'

((((((DO THE MATH))))))

`COMBINING 'EVERYONES' HEAVY HEART BREAKING $PERSONAL LOSSES$ "ETC". -
EVERYTHING FROM THE WAR ZONE HURRICANES, TO THE DEVASTATING CALIF- FIRES;
TOSS IN THE LAS VEGAS SHOOTER! - WHO DIDN'T GET TO EXAMINE MY (MEDIA BANNED)
'SHOWSTOPPER' MEMO. THEREFORE, WHAT YOU GOT TO BE ASKING YOURSELVES 'IS, WAS
IT ALL $WORTH IT??? 'TO DENIE MY 'LIVE WIRE PRAYERS 'BEING ANSWERED; THUS
SENT FORTH FROM GOD'S REVOLUTIONARY, EDUCATIONAL WORD! - OR 'END OF DAZE ON
BORROWED TIME! - SIGNED: FAITH BASED MESSENGER TO THE MASSES... ARMAGEDDON
'Life' *according to* A LARGE SCALE WEATHER PREVAILING ENVIRONMENT. TO YOU YET!?

IN BRIEF: STARTING FROM' THE BRAZILIAN PLACEBO GOD , WORSHIPING,
SONWORLD THE REDEEMER, ELECTRO FINGER BLAST OFF'ZIKA VIRUS'EXHIBIT.
ONE WILL FIND godzilla THE NEGATIVE ATMO-SPIRIT HOVERING OVER TO
ACCOMMODATE YOU! - FOR NAME SAKE GODZILLA LOVES TO HANG OUT IN THE SO
CALLED HOLY LAND!!! FUKUSHIMA **DEMONIC DISASTER** ? FOR ALL I KNOW, ONE
COULD HAVE BEEN PRAYING DIRECTLY TO SOME HUGE 'REPLACEMENT FALSE God
BUDDHA STATUE, IN THEIR' OWN BACK YARD.

"END OF DAZE, SIGNED: YOURS TRULY, OFFICIAL ✓ 'NEGATIVE SPIRIT BUSTER"
COMMON KNOWLEDGE IS TO KNOW GOD LOVES YOU, AND THAT GOD IS FORGIVING;
IN THAT TO CLAIM THE REALITY OF MORAL RELIGIOUS CONVICTION,
IS IN ALWAYS BEING WORTHY OF GOD'S LOVE.

"Presenting GOD'S INSPIRED WORD." (44)

FRIAR FLYER

'THIS WEEK'S SERMON'
'BY THE MONK AMONG YOU'

'THESIS-CHRIST PEOPLE'

OCT.31ST
RIGHT
N.Y.C.

DO THE MATH

(2017) COMBINING 'EVERYONES' HEAVY HEART BREAKING $PERSONAL LOSSES$ "ETC". -
EVERYTHING FROM THE WAR ZONE HURRICANES, TO THE DEVASTATING CALIF- FIRES;
TOSS IN THE LAS VEGAS SHOOTER! - WHO DIDN'T GET TO EXAMINE MY (MEDIA BANNED)
'SHOWSTOPPER' MEMO. THEREFORE, WHAT YOU GOT TO BE ASKING YOURSELVES 'IS WAS,
IT ALL $WORTH IT??? 'TO DENIE MY 'LIVE WIRE PRAYERS 'BEING ANSWERED; THUS
SENT FORTH FROM GOD'S REVOLUTIONARY, EDUCATIONAL WORD! - OR 'END OF DAZE ON
BORROWED TIME!!!

There's no misinterpreting 'Meaning'

FURTHERMORE, PROOF THEREOF' BY WAY OF THESE PURPOSEFUL FONTS DESIGNED BY GOD.
- WORKING THRU YOURS TRULY. 'ALWAYS REMEMBER, I'M NOT DOING THIS FOR MY HEALTH
AND WELL'BEING, I'M DOING THIS FOR YOU, AND YOURS. WHEREAS TO IGNORE THESE
PERIODICALLY SENT FORTH, GOD'S RECHERCHE' EDUCATIONAL WORD, IS NOT TO BE TAKEN
LIGHTLY; OR IMPROPERLY DISPOSED OF. 'AS WHY THIS IS WHAT HAPPENED WITH THESE
FORETOLD STORIES IN RETROSPECT, 'RESULTING IN' = godZILLA = THE REAL ESTATE =
DESTROYER = FILLING IN THE AVAILABLE GAP BY WAY OF CAUSING ALL THIS HORRENDOUS
DEATH AND DESTRUCTION. 'ATMOSPHERIC 'POSITIVE (VERSUS) 'ATMOSPHERIC 'NEGATIVE.
'ONLY GOODNESS COMES FROM GOD! 'STARTING OVER WITH YOU, AND YOURS PROTECTION
ANYONE??? SIGNED: 'TELL ALL' IN YOUR FACE, CLASS ROOM SAVIOR OF THE WORLD...
WHAT'S TRENDING? SCOOP ON OPIOIDS, OR ILLICIT DRUGS! T-SHIRT ANYONE? THE REASON
THEY CALL IT 'DOPE' IS THAT NOBODY INTELLIGENT IS TAKING IT. 'SEPARATION FROM
REAL AND FAKE'. THEREFORE, 'GET A LIFE, DON'T FORFIT YOURS... IN BRIEF:
TALKING POINTS! 'NOSTRIL-DAMUS, PREDICTS THAT THE BEST WAY TO CURB THE 'OVER
USAGE OF THE EXPRESSION 'MISERY LOVES COMPANY' IS IN PROVIDING ADEQUATE GLOBAL
BIRTH CONTROL...

" When words need to be said "
The Future of earth balance democracy is at stake.

You say you want a revolution?

'THIS IS AMERICA'.

THIS CLASSROOM CONNECTION IS BROUGHT TO YOU BY, 'PEN NAME' DR.
SUNDAY, 1980 FOUNDER, OF 'THE POSITIVE FAITH 'ONE WORLD' RELIGION.
'SEEK AND YOU SHALL FIND = THIS HERE BEING A "CRY WOLF" DISCOVERY KIT OF
L.M.T. 89503...

'Life' according to (New-age) Catechism Lessons.

"ALL POSITIVE GOD, WOULD 'NEVER! SUGGEST NEGATIVITY INTO ONE'S MIND."

Own A Moment In Time

BASED ON A ANCIENT BIBLICAL, BELIEF SYSTEM THAT GOD TOLD ABRAHAM, TO TAKE THA LIFE OF ABE'S SON IN A RITUAL SACRIFICE. - THEN IT PENED! READING BETWEEN THA LINES IN REALITY IS AN UNEXPLAINED DUEL SPIRITUAL CONFRONTATION THAT WENT ON.
✳ GOD, THE POSITIVE SPIRIT, THE HOLY SPIRIT, WOULD NEVER MINDFULLY SUGGEST TO ANYONE, THIS KIND OF NEGATIVE DELUSIONAL BEHAVIOR, IN THA FIRST PLACE. IN RETROSPECT THIS WEAK-MINDED DEFENDANT WAS DANCING TO THA INVASION OF A NEGATIVE SUGGESTIVE THOUGHT CONCEPT., OR IF YOU WILL, THA BEAST IN MAN,
AND ✳ GOD PREVAILED... **New gospel** THEORY

"DUBYA, ON FAITH BASED INITIATIVE,. WE WELCOME **All** FAITHS IN AMERICA." YEAH RIGHT !/ CONTESTABLY SPEAKING, FOR GOODNESS SNAKE. ADAM & EVE, WEREN'T THA FIRST TWO PEOPLE ON EARTH., MOST LIKELY THEY WERE THA FIRST TWO LITERATE PEOPLE THAT HAD THA CHANCE TO PASS ALONG THEIR STORIES! AS THA STORY GOES EDEN AWAY AT HIS HEART, SOCIABLY ADAM RIBBED EVE INTO SPENDING THA WEEKEND AT A LOCAL NUDIST CAMP. ONCE THEY GOT IN THERE SHE REALIZED SHE, WAS THA APPLE OF HIS EYE. EVE THEN TRIED TO ENTICE HIM INTO TAKING AN ILLEGAL SUBSTANCE OF SNAKE PUSHER OPIOIDS! TOTALLY FREAKED, HE RAN OVER AND PUT ON HIS CAMP FORBIDDEN FRUIT OF THA LOOM SKIVVIES, AND THEY BOTH GOT **86**, PARADISE...

"GREAT BIBLICAL INTERPRETATIONS"

This is not your father's religion.

CHART YOUR COURSE TO a Better

improvement OF INTERNATIONAL history

(46)

PSYCHOLOGY ON ORDER:

Questions about questions

Globalizing big ideas

FROM HERE TO THERE

SOME OF THE BRIGHTEST LEGAL MINDS
NEVER WENT TO LAW SCHOOL.

NEWS OF RECORD on **NATIONWIDE Gunman** GONE WILD,

"THE SHOOTER:

"IF YOU BUILD THIS THEY WILL COME"
'OR'

- JUST ANOTHER WALK IN THE PARK OF 'END OF DAZE ON
BORROWED TIME' FEATHER RUFFLING, 'BUSINESS AS USUAL

Vintage Journalism •

THE FOCUS GROUP THAT ACTUALLY FOCUSED ?

'DISCOUNT BABY'

HERE'S THE BEEF !

The Fight for The Right to Preach.

When a man lives to help others

IT'S NO SECRET

EVIL NEEDS TO BE AFRAID

BETTER LIVING THROUGH DISCOVERY

FINALLY... LIFE INSURANCE YOU CAN AFFORD.

'WAKE UP AND SMELL THE C-O-P-Y' OF **A Democracy Prison Original**,

By YOURS TRULY, THE LEGEND OF ANYWHERE **but Here** FREE Speech!

SIMPLY

A little book full of BIG wisdom.

A BRIGHTER TOMORROW IS COMING!

Spreading THE Word ON

HOW TO INJECT MATURITY AND RESPONSIBILITY INTO CHILDREN.

47½

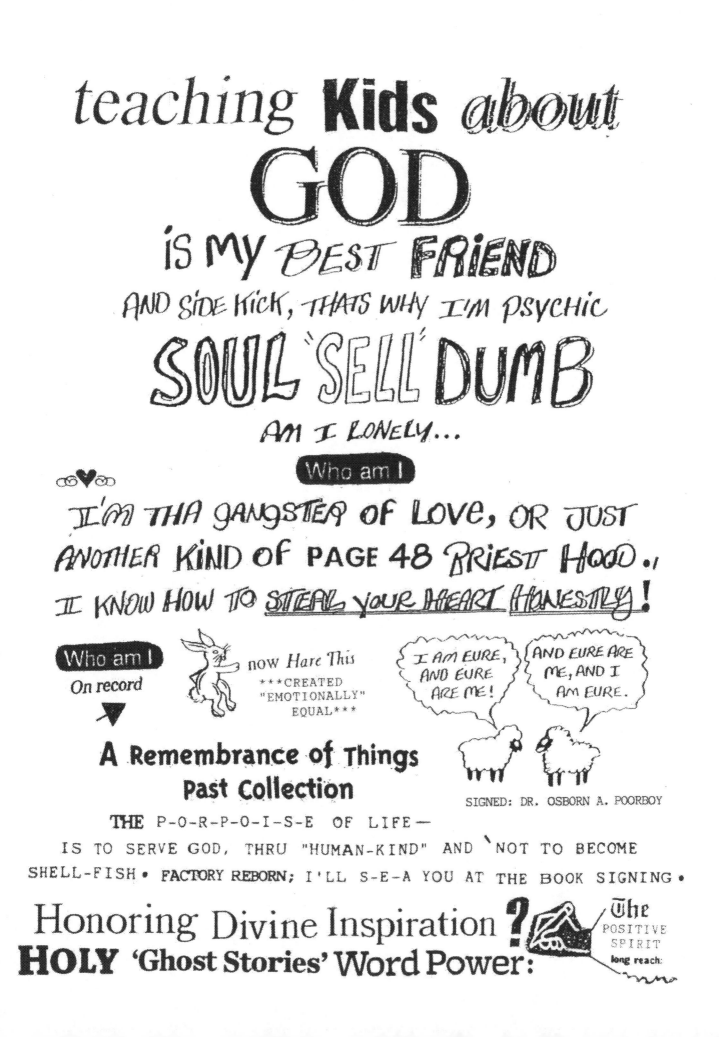

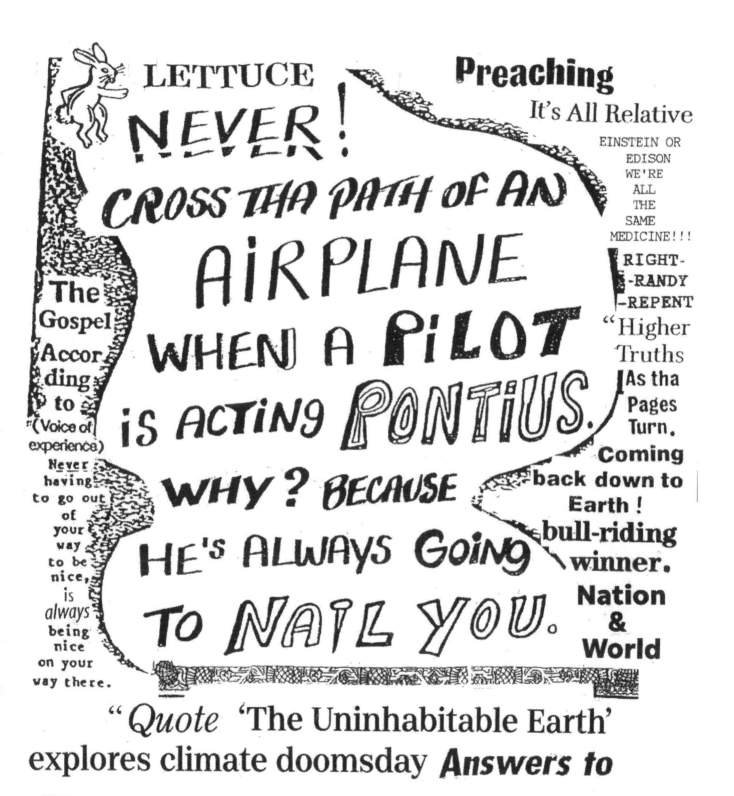

LETTUCE

NEVER!
CROSS THA PATH OF AN AIRPLANE WHEN A **PiLOT** is ACTing **PONTIUS.** WHY? BECAUSE HE'S ALWAYS GOING TO NAIL YOU.

Preaching
It's All Relative

EINSTEIN OR EDISON WE'RE ALL THE SAME MEDICINE!!!

RIGHT-
-RANDY
-REPENT

"Higher Truths As tha Pages Turn.

Coming back down to Earth! bull-riding winner.

Nation & World

The Gospel According to "(Voice of experience)

Never having to go out of your way to be nice, is always being nice on your way there.

" *Quote* 'The Uninhabitable Earth' explores climate doomsday **Answers to**

EVERYTHING IN LIFE IS TO A DEGREE!'OCEAN BATH WATER; MASSIVE FOSSIL FUEL USAGE; ALONG WITH CONTRIBUTING TO A OVER-POPULATION WANTS & NEEDS... 'DO YOU KNOW WHAT THE 'CALL IN' SUICIDE PREVENTION CLINIC'S 'STAY ALIVE' PHILOSOPHICAL RESPONSE IS ??? "THERE'S ALWAYS SOMEBODY OUT THERE THAT'S WORSE OFF THAN YOU"... ☺ (49)

Just when you thought you'd seen everything!
Writer traces roots of religion

"R-E-A-D-I-N-G-B-E-T-W-E-E-N-T-H-E-L-I-N-E-S"

"IN THIS MAN'S RELIGION THERE'S GOD IN MAN,
BUT THERE'S NO SUCH THING AS A MAN THAT'S GOD!"

Facing Up to Reality
Bible **Deciphering** reform to
THE ONE and only GOD.

"always on call" INTRODUCING **INSTANT TELLER.** Here's the one OF **ALL** GOD

EVIDENCE OF TITLE

The one and only ORIGINAL.

Form 1040EZ **Instructions for preparing**

STRAIGHTFORWARD **Miracle** WORKING "?

'*Revelation*'

This is about tha only
yours to use AUTHENTIC
portrayal OF
The **INSTANT TELLER,**
you stand to gain by.

"BEFORE I CREATED YOU GUYS; WHEN I WAS YOUNG
I, CREATED THA DINOSAURS JUST SO THAT I COULD
HAVE SOME TOYS TO PLAY WITH"...

The Positive 'SPIRIT
'Without GENDER.

PROVIDED FOR YOUR PROTECTION.

*FLESH AND BLOOD MAN
IS ONLY MAN, MAID* (50)
IN THA IMAGE AND LIKENESS OF ONESELF.

IN THE SPOTLIGHT

'I'M NOT PARTICULARLY FOND OF ALL THOSE PEOPLE OUT THERE THAT CLAIM TO HAVE MORE MONEY THAN ME! - MAYBE I'LL JUST HAVE TO GO OUT THERE AND GET MYSELF, MY OWN TV, SHOW! - AFTER ALL, "I'M THE BEST TEACHER" - I HOME-SCHOOLED THE BEST OF DR. SUNDAY. - JUST THE SAME 'FOR NOW' I'LL BE OK WITH 'CAMEO STEALING' ALL THE LIME LIGHT ON THE DR. SUNDAY SHOW; 'I'M A TOUGH ACT TO FOLLOW...

'WANTED: A SIGNIFICANT SOUNDING GENDERLESS' SPEAKING VOICE, FOR THE VOICE OF GOD! GENERAL INFO: "BASED ON THIS BOOK'S SCRIPTURE" THERE'S THINGS THAT GOD WOULD SAY; AND THINGS THAT GOD WOULD NEVER SAY; THERE'S THINGS THAT GOD WOULD DO; AND THINGS THAT GOD WOULD NEVER DO... SIGNED: YOURS TRULY, 'A GENIUS CONTROLER.

READY FOR PRIME TIME
we need God in our lives.

PROPITIOUSLY AN EQUAL OPPERTUNITY EMPLOYER, THE Positive spirit, **PRESCRIPTION STRENGTH** WITHIN, Sheds Light on the Body of the Beholder!.
HOLY 'Ghost Stories' Word Power:
"Presenting GOD'S INSPIRED WORD."
'ONLY GOODNESS COMES FROM GOD'.

'LET POSITIVITY TRULY REIGN'

GOSPEL FICTIONS
REFORM TAKES SHAPE
A Straight Look at Questions That Linger,

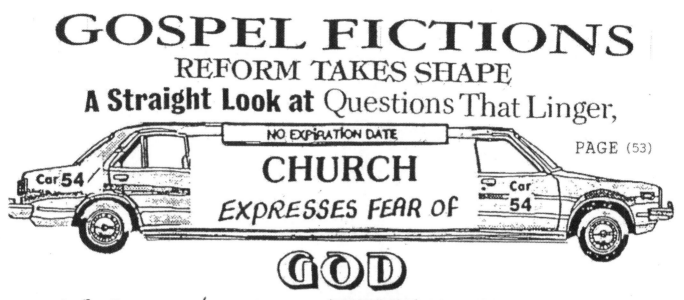

NO EXPIRATION DATE
CHURCH
EXPRESSES FEAR OF
Car 54
Car 54

GOD

OR GOD-FEARING PEOPLE. **Beyond tha Scare** replaced by New gospel THEORY POSITIVE RAIN, NEGATIVE RAIN!

IF YOU SHOULD ASK ME! HOW CAN THERE BE ANY FEAR of GOD, WHEN IN FACT ALL THA GOOD MOR-PHOLOGICAL ELEMENTS of ENJOYABLE LIFE AND HUMANISTIC RELATIONSHIPS, CAN ONLY BE ATTRI-BUTED TO THE ALWAYS WAS, AND ALWAYS WILL BE, ATMOSPIRIT WORKING POSITIVE. THE

POSITIVE Spirit COMETH Teaching of New Age TRUTHS.

foresight **IM PRUV ALL** written OPINION COMMENTARY.

Give 'em some of that 'new-time religion'

APRIL 24th, 2013 IN THE NEWS: A COUPLE BELONGING TO A FUNDAMENTALIST CHRISTIAN CHURCH THAT BELIEVES IN FAITH HEALING, SERVING PROBATION FOR THE 2009 DEATH OF THEIR TODDLER AFTER THEY TURNED TO PRAYER INSTEAD OF A DOCTOR, COULD FACE NEW CHARGES NOW THAT ANOTHER SON HAS DIED". 'BEHOLD THE TESTIMONY' IN HEARING OUR PRAYERS! GOD'S CREATED DOCTORS - VIA - 'GOD GIVEN TALENT' TO CURE OUR ILL'S! WHEREBY WITH RECURRING MULTITUDES OF (POSITIVE) RESULTS THEREOF. - FURTHERMORE 'REALISTIC FIGURE OF SPEACH ENDS TRAVESTY' WHEREAS 'ONLY TRUTH CAN FREE YOU'. YOURS TRULY, THE PUBLIC SERPENT OR CHARMING SNAKE, THAT WOULD TAKE THE BITE OUT OF SHADY 'RELIGION AND SERUM IN THE RIGHT

GOSPEL ACCORDING TO A 'Spiritual Awakening'.

SIGNED: THE SNAKE THAT DOESN'T DO GRASS...

Ancient Sunni-Shiite divide
discussion in moral terms
~Quran/
RIGHT WHERE THEY LEFT OFF
Doctor's Shocking Revelation
"FEATURING SECTARIAN RACISM"

A lot of people won't even realize the truth of the situation until you point it out.

(((LABELED AS RACISM)))

MOSQUE MADNESS, 'REPAIR KIT' '72 VERSIONS OF "ONLY TRUTH CAN FREE YOU"!

'STRATEGY' THAT SHOULD BE HIGHLY CONSIDERED!!!

The art of restoring magnetic heads — People,

to be a card carrying member of the 'true family of ALLAH;

there are no ethnical RACE, CREED, OR COLOR, **differences** •

"WHEREAS TO FIND 'POSITIVE SAMENESS' WITHIN YOUR FELLOW MAN 'IS TO FIND HEAVEN ON EARTH' S-A-N-E-N-E-S-S = AMEN "

Introducing **The world according to** THE 'MAHDI'

♫ COME TOGETHER RIGHT NOW, OVER ME...

The book on 'Remove all doubt'
NO LOOKING BACK. PAGE (54)

WORLD'S #1 CONDITIONER

"BOOK'S PARALLEL EPILOGUE: AND DEAR GOD, NO NEED TO FORGIVE ANYONE NOW = FOR THEY KNOW NOW WHAT THEY DO!".

FAITH FORUM QUESTION ON:

MOST INSPIRING RELIGIOUS FIGURE? ANSWERS TO

" ALL THIS HASN'T BEEN GIVEN TO ME FOR NOTHING."

5 MINUTES TO FREEDOM
LET US COUNT THE WAY
Powerful Testimony: PUBLIC — FOR — UM

J LOSING THEIR RELIGION AND GAINING MINE???
'THUS BECOMES MERGERS FINEST HOUR!!!

((Biblical Correctness)) *Teaching of* New Age *TRUTHS.*

THERE'S only one **GOD** THE POSITIVE **Spirit.**

World must face truth,

THE POSITIVE **Spirit** COMETH.

A Straight Look at Questions That Linger.

*FLESH AND BLOOD MAN IS ONLY MAN, MAID
IN THA IMAGE AND LIKENESS OF ONESELF.*

DECODING THA **TRINITY** *3 AMIGOS* Term Limits.

Say It Ain't So, enjoy your retirement PAGE.

Reality Check ⌐reform⌐ Tha Party's Over. ☺

DOCTOR'S BOOK OF NEW World **REMEDIES**

bull-riding winner spreads views

Guidelines: "PEACEFUL 'EVOLUTION, REVOLUTION,
IS THE SOLUTION TO BE FREE OF MENTAL POLUTION."

""PRODUCTS OF OUR ENVIRONMENT""
HUMAN BEANS, PLANTED SEEDS, POTENTIAL ANYTHINGS,
'WITHOUT POSITIVE DOMINANT FEEDBACK...

'THY WILL BE DONE' APPOINTMENT REMINDER'
OUTTA THIS WORLD AND ON WITH THE NEXT??

((ANSWERS TO MYSTERIOUS END OF AN AGE PROPHECY FULFILLED))
A MEDIA POSTED, OR PUBLICIZED GATHERING EVENT???

WILD HORSES COULDN'T DRAG ME AWAY

'HOW TO MAKE A POINT AT THE SPEED OF LIGHT'?

"THE 'NEW WORLD' BEGINS IN YOUR OWN BACKYARD"!!!

(55)

"RAJAN ZED **FAITH FORUM** / **RENO GAZETTE-JOURNAL.**"
Sunday, June 17, 2012

If God is everywhere, why go to worship?

TODAY'S QUICK READ

DR.SUNDAY,
HOW IN THE HELL DO YOU EXPECT US TO MAKE ANY MONEY? - ONLY KIDDING! ☺

ANSWERS TO: THE REASSURANCE OF 'FAITH BASED' SOLIDARITY!!!

FAITH FORUM Sunday, January 29, 2017

If you could ask Pope Francis anything, what would it be?

HOW WOULD YOU LIKE TO BECOME MY VICE PRESIDENT OF RELIGION, ALONG WITH ALL OF YOUR 1.2 BILLION FOLLOWERS COMING ALONG FOR THE RIDE? - THE BAD NEWS IS THAT YOUR GOING TO HAVE TO TEACH YOUR 'OLD DOG-MA NEW TRICKS! THE GOOD NEWS IS THAT YOUR GOING TO HAVE TO ADOPT MY DOG-MA; SHE'S A REAL GOOD 'CONVERT RETRIEVER' TO ` MY RELIGION!

FAITH FORUM

Does art of dying well apply to all?

NOT IF IT'S AT THE HANDS OF SADISTIC ISIS, OR A DRUNK DRIVER, ETC."ETC"
'FURTHERMORE WE'RE ALL VISITORS OF THIS PLANET PLAN IT; "WE'RE ALL SNOWMEN UNDER SUNLAMPS; WE ALL LIVE TO BE SOMEBODIES MEMORIES; BIRTH IS TERMINAL; AND NOBODY GET'S OUT OF THIS WORLD ALIVE"...

Has the market become God?

'ONLY WHEN THEY HAVE ASPARAGUS ON SALE!!!

Does 'prayer' bring concrete, quantifiable results?

'IF YOU'RE WORKING AT A PROSPEROUS CEMENT FACTORY IT DOES!

ALL CONTRIBUTING

(EXAMPLE) 'A P.T.S.D NIGHTMARE SWITCH AND BATE REMEDY? - LISTEN TO MUSIC A GOOD PORTION OF THE DAY, AND OR NIGHT, AND CHANCES ARE ONE OF THOSE CATCHY SONGS YOU LIKE OR NOT, HAUNTINGLY WILL 'BRAIN WORM' BE PLAYING OVER AND OVER AGAIN IN YOUR HEAD AS YOU SLEEP; AS OPPOSED TO THE CONTRARY. (EXAMPLE) - AS LIKE WHAT I WROTE ABOUT SNIPER KYLE, IN TWITTER - HE SHOULD HAVE TAKEN HIS KILLER TO DISNEYLAND "ETC" AS OPPOSED TO P.T.S.D LAND. 'OR (EXAMPLE) WATCH FREQUENTLY 2 HRS, OF OLD SCHOOL 3 STOOGES FILMS, AT NIGHT BEFORE YOU GO TO BED; AND YOU'LL WAKE UP IN THE MORNING WANTING TO BECOME A ROCKET SCIENTIST. WHERE-AS, IT'S 'HOW ONE' KEEPS P.T.S.D ON A 'NEVER ADVANCING BACK BURNER.
FURTHERMORE, SHOULD YOU SUGGEST THE 'RESPONSIBILITY OF PET ADOPTION PRICELESS.

We've got issues.

☞ TO MAKE'UM THINK, IS TO MAKE'UM BLINK! 'IRAN, ALWAYS REMEMBER IN USING A NUKE YOU GET 5, MINUTES OF NEW YEAR'S EVE CELEBRATION; THEN IT'S YOUR TURN TO BURN... 3/15
SIGNED: AYATOLL-YA-SO, HUMANELY ☺

(56)

NOTICE IS HEREBY GIVEN THE **Positive** Spirit COMETH...

1980 *foundation of God's new world* by DR. Sunday.

HOW TO CAPTURE

The Positive Spirit, INNERSOUL SUPPORT SYSTEM ,.

worldwide A Gospel SPECIAL **Culture** *Harvest* HEINZ

 Reinventing **THE** CHURCH

page 57 *Varieties*

learning to know, love and serve God.

100% GUARANTEE INSPIRATION *works for me."*

DO NOT ENTER FOR MAN'S SAKE, BUT FOR 'GOD SAKE ENTER.

THIS IS THA CHURCH OF "THE" ONE AND ONLY. WHERE THA RESPONDENTS NEVER LEAVE LONELY. JUST A MASS OF UNDERSTANDING TO BE IN UNION WITH THE COMMUNION OF HAPPY THOUGHTS. WHEREBY, THIS IS IN THA ART OF REASONING TO THE **Positive** TO BE of INNER PEACE of **MIND**.

Who Speaks For God?
Need a new roommate!
INVISIBLE GUIDING INNERSOUL SUPPORT SYSTEM

'THE POSITIVE SPIRIT, GHOSTWRITER.

THIS BOOK SPEAKS VOLUMES ...

'WORD ON' LEGENDARY MAVERICK 'PREACHER YOURS TRULY, "SANITY CLAUSE"

"for I am no better than any human –kind person – in any human-kind situation "

= Speaks volumes.) WALK IN MY SHOES P–L–E–A–S–E.

Could a 'Book of Trump' go into the Bible?

'NOT ACCORDING TO' PATRIOT EXTRAORDINAR, YOURS TRULY!!!

The USA Today Network 'SHOULD HAVE' **reached out to** THIS **expert**.

`WELCOME ABOARD 'MOD SQUAD LADIES;

SINCE WHEN DID PRES. TRUMP PURCHASE THIS COUNTRY???

"THIS LAND IS YOUR LAND; THIS LAND IS MY LAND, ETC. ♫

WHAT EVER HAPPENED TO 'UNITED WE STAND; DIVIDED WE FALL"?

GOSPEL ACCORDING TO "YOU CAN'T HANDLE THE TRUTH.

- TO BE ORDAINED INTO THIS MAN'S RELIGION IS TO BE ABLE TO: 'CAN YOU SAY' INCLUDING ONESELF!

"I TRULY LOVE EVERY WELL BEHAVED PERSON ON THE PLANET".

NEXT: **FAITH FORUM** "PRES. TRUMP,

Is tax evasion a sin in God's eyes? ☺

Next up **on** Tell-all book :

'A HISTORIC MOMENT'

SIMPLIFIED

deep thoughts on political issues

Opinion

Impeachment central

'IT WAS A WITCH HUNT WITH A 400 MILLION DOLLAR SMOKING BROOM STICK;
THAT HAD A 'OBVIOUS OUTCOME' TO THIS POLITICAL THEATER; THUS IN
CONCLUSION: $STICKING IT TO THE TAX PAYER...

DR. Sunday   *FRIAR FLYER*   NEWSLETTERCOMMENTARY

He is 'NOT DEMOCRACY PRIVILEGE **born.**

yet **Wise Men Still Seek Him.**

(58)

Should we preach politics from the pulpit?

MORAL COMPASS THIS! - WHEN INCUMBENT POLITICAL SOCIETY IS'
PREACHING QUACKERY; THERE NEEDS TO BE A CHECKS AND BALANCES,
OUTLET COMING FROM SOMEWHERE. - THEREFORE, OF THE PEOPLE, BY
THE PEOPLE, FOR THE PEOPLE, REVERTS BACK TO HERE.- BESIDES WHEN YOUR
THE AUTHOR OF 'THE GOSPEL ACCORDING TO RELIGION AND POLITICS'
PROFOUNDLY' SERMON CITY IS INEVITABLE...

FAITH FORUM # How has God helped you through troubled times?

THOU SHELT NOT 'KILL IS TATOOED ON MY SOUL! WHEN I GOT
DRAFTED INTO THE U.S. ARMY; I FELT AS IF GOD HAD ABANDON
ME; WHEREAS, I HAD NO DESIRE TO GO TO VIETNAM AND START
KILLING PEOPLE THAT I HAD NOTHING AGAINST, AND FOR NO
'REAL REASON' AT ALL! (((PULLING STRINGS GOD TO THE RES-
CUE))). 'SO WHEN IT CAME TIME FOR ME TO BOARD THE PLANE
TO GO THERE; I CAME DOWN WITH PNEUMONIA, AND A 103 TEMP;
I BECAME DELIRIOUS; AND ALL THE HOSPITAL STAFF LOOKED LIKE
THEY WERE ALL WALKING AROUND WEARING MICKEY MOUSE HEADS; SO
I DUCKED UNDER THE COVERS! - "I NEVER ENDED UP GOING TO
VIETNAM". FURTHERMORE, LACKING ANY GUNG-HO ENTHUSIASM,
WHEN IT CAME TIME FOR ME TO DO MY WEAPONS TESTING; I SHOT
AT THE GUY NEXT TO ME'S TARGET, AND BY THAT AFTERNOON HE,
WAS ON HIS WAY TO VIETNAM! - SO WHEN IT CAME TIME FOR ME
TO PICK UP MY SHOOTING RANGE MEDAL, THEY HANDED ME THE
SHARP SHOOTERS MEDAL 'CAUSE THEY TOLD ME THAT THEY HAD
RAN OUT OF 'MARKSMAN' - MEDALS, AS WAS STATED TO ME LIKE
THAT...

BACK FOR MORE

FAITH FORUM # Why should we love God?

"GREAT BIBLICAL INTERPRETATIONS"

'ONLY GOODNESS COMES FROM GOD'.

Discover a New Dimension in Learning
GETTING IT RIGHT.

VALIDATION TIME FOR

'REVOLUTIONARY PREACHER'

"I WAS RAISED TO RESPECT MY ELDERS 'BUT
WHEN IT COMES TO BEING CONFRONTED WITH
NEANDERTHALISM?! - WRITTEN BY MAN,
INSPIRED BY GOD: IS 'NOW
HOT OFF THE PRESS"...

Greatest show on Earth campaign

UNIVERSAL Faith Reformation !

"THIS HERE BEING A 'PEACE ON EARTH,'ONE WORLD RELIGION' PROPOSAL"

'RIGHTEOUSLY COMBATING MADNESS'

Lessons learned from failure.

A MAN HAS GOT TO KNOW 'HIS <u>SAME PAGE</u>
RELIGIOUS LIMITATIONS OR THE WHOLE WORLD
JUST ALL BECOMES A 'GO TO HELL SOCIETY!

BIG-TIME INSPIRATION

"This is what 'I was put on earth to do".

bull-riding winner

♫ *TO MANY CHURCHS, AND NOT ENOUGH TRUTH!* ♫

R.G.J
FAITH FORUM QUESTION ON:

MOST INSPIRING RELIGIOUS FIGURE?

" ALL THIS HASN'T BEEN GIVEN TO ME FOR NOTHING."

Give 'em some of that '<u>new</u>-time religion. ♫♫ (60)

FRIAR FLYER "The world according to *The*
CHOSEN ONE MESSIAH, CLASSROOM SAVIOR OF THE WORLD."

VICTIM'S OUTRAGE defends legal brothels

- ACCORDING TO PRES. TRUMP, WHO STATES HIS MAIN CONCERN FOR BUILDING THE $WALL IS TO STOP DRUG TRAFFICKING VIA IF IT TAKES HAVING TO ROB PETER TO PAY PAUL, TO DO IT. WHEREAS, IF THE DRUG CARTEL CAN TUNNEL DIG EL-CHAPO OUT OF JAIL; THEY CAN NO PROBLEM DIG UNDER THOSE WALLS. FURTHERMORE, ONE CAN CATAPULT, OR THROW BUNDLES OF DRUGS OVER TO THE OTHER SIDE, TO SOME GUY WEARING A SOMBRERO AND ANSWERING TO THE NAME OF 'COMBO PLATE SPECIAL' ☺ 'IN THE NEWS' IN AS FAR AS OVER-ALL HEALTH-CARE IS CONCERN; - WITH THE GOVERNMENT'S LACK OF 'SYMMETRY, WE'RE ALL THAT MUCH CLOSER TO THE 'CEMETERY!!! ☺ BOEING; - WHO EVER DESIGNED THAT TAKE-OFF FLIGHT PLAN MYSTERY SHIFT HAVE A GOOD ONE FIASCO; 'SHOULD GET LIFE IN PRISON! - WITH NO CABLE, OR QU-ALITY MEDICAL 'ETC - KIND OF LIKE HOW I LIVE MY LIFE AS A COMMON FOLK CITIZEN... 'CATHOLIC SCHOOL NATION: 'IN BRIEF' THE DIME A DOZEN CHURCH PEDOPHILE PRIEST "ETC" NEVER REALLY BOUGHT INTO PLACEBO - GOD - JESUS! - THUS IN HAVING TO PROMOTE THIS SCAM FOR—THEIR' YOUR OK, I'M OK, EMPLOYER; GIVING THEM THE 'EXCUSE THEY NEEDED TO BECOME AUTHORITATIVE PEDOPHILIES. WHEREAS, ANYONE WHO EVER TRULY LOVES GOD, WOULD 'NEVER DO ANYTHING LIKE THAT, OR EVEN THINK THAT WAY! - THEREFORE, WE' NEED TO OBLITERATE' ALL THOSE 'DEVIL IN THE DETAILS' CHILD PORN 'PRAYER BOOKS' ETC... IN REFERENCE TO SEN. McSALLY'S TRAGIC RAPE TESTIMONY! - APPALLING TO ME; "I BELIEVE THAT 'ALL SEX SHOULD BE CONSENSUAL". - OFFICER DICK HEAD, AND ALL OF HIS MILITARY NATIONWIDE COHORTS FROM THIS LOW-LIFER EPIDEMIC; 'NEED A VIABLE OPTION' THAT LEADS TO CONSENSUAL! 'EVERY - COWARD' HAS A SILVER LINING! - "EXAMPLE IN BRIEF" CURBING THIS INSANITY IN THE REALM OF MILITARY FACILITIES; LET THERE BE A MRS.ROBINSON COUGAR, CAT-HOUSE $25 DOLLARS A DANCE, THANKING THEM FOR THEIR SERVICE; AS OPPOSED TO DISGRACING THEM FOR IT. THIS HERE BEING THE DIFFERENCE IN ONE GETTING A HONORABLE DISCHARGE IN MORE WAYS THAN ONE... 'CHEATING IN SCHOOL IS A PERFECT EXAMPLE OF ONE, CHEATING ONESELF, OUT OF AN EDUCATION. ☺ 'IN CONCLUSION OF THIS HERE ESSAY FLYER; "MY" DISCOVERY BECOMES THE MOST NOTABLE EVENT EVER TO TAKE PLACE IN THE HISTORY OF 'ALL MAN'KIND...

'FINALLY'
A VIABLE LOBBYIST FOR

GOD

THAT

jolts Washington into
RESPONSIBILITY!

Reassuring POWER TO THE PEOPLE,.
Political football: Half Time at *The* Revolution PAGE (61)

Crime & Punishment
'Time for small thinking is over,'
"Open Season on Common Folk Citizens"
Orlando, San Bernardino, Fresno, next???
CRITICAL THINKERS (READ) **what you've been missing.**

Showstopper becomes 'your call if you want it to be"

LEAVE YOU WITH ONE SIMPLE THOUGHT:
VICTIM'S OUTRAGE
project

"ALL MURDERERS SHALL BE SET FREE."

HELL'S ESCALATION, OR REHABILITATION CITY IS A TOWN WITHOUT PITY. SO LET ME HIP YOU BEFORE WE SHIP YOU... IN FUTURE WORLD GAMES LET A MURDERER SWIM HOME FROM THA MIDDLE OF THA OCEAN TO PROVE THEIR NOT UNJUST PRE-MEDITATED, SPONTANEOUS, INSANE DEATH CER-TIFICATE HOLDERS, BUT INCOMPETENT SWIM-MERS THROUGH NO FAULT OF THE SYSTEM. IN CONJUNCTION, THA SHORT CHANGING OF A IGNOMINIOUS ONE'S LIFE EXPECTANCY., TENACIOUSLY DOING UN TO OTHERS, FOR THA GAMES MUST GO ON.

"PEOPLE BURGERS MY FAVORITE!"

"SIN-FULLY DELICIOUS"

""PRODUCTS OF OUR ENVIRONMENT""
HUMAN BEANS, PLANTED SEEDS, POTENTIAL ANYTHINGS,
'WITHOUT POSITIVE DOMINANT FEEDBACK...

Time Out!

: A LUCKY DAY FOR SOME :

- WITH 'ALL THE LOW-LIFE HORRIFIC CRIMINALS THAT OVER THE YEARS CAME ALONG AND I WROTE ABOUT; I BROKE THIS DOWN TO A LIMITED AMOUNT OF STORY TELLING ANALYSIS TO JUST A FEW, NOT TO MENTION IN THE MONOGRAPH, THE WARP MINDED NORWEGIAN RACIST, WHO GUN DOWN 77. - THE WARP MINDED NEW ZEALAND RACIST, WHO GUN DOWN 50. - AND LAST BUT NOT LEAST, THE WARP MINDED GERMAN, 'DEVIL IS MY CO-PILOT' WHO DELIBERATELY CRASHED A PLANE LOAD OF PEOPLE INTO A MOUNTAIN. - ENCAPSULATING, CONSEQUENCES, DETERENT PROPOSAL! - MECCA WEST (HELL) AWAITS THEIR DELIVERY!!! - AS THE STORY GOES...

(62)

"Storytelling on a grand scale"
THE POSITIVE Faith Religion
Laying Claim to Ministry of Higher Education ...
WELCOME TO *The* formation of a conscience

=== TO MAKE'UM THINK, IS TO MAKE'UM BLINK! ===

'A MENTAL HEALTH CARE, OBLIGATORY 'TEACHABLE MOMENT;
'ON A MISSION FROM GODZILLA; WAKE-UP CALL, ACTION-STOPPER!!!
(((((("ONLY TRUTH CAN FREE YOU"))))))
"QUOTE" (ZEPPELIN SONG) ♫ I REALLY WANT TO KNOW; HOW MUCH THERE IS TO KNOW?

Discover a New Dimension in Learning
GETTING IT RIGHT.

ALL CONTRIBUTING TO A contagious-philosophy *exemplifies* What you need to know **AND** Process.

"GREAT BIBLICAL INTERPRETATIONS"

This is not your father's religion ●

❝ THE NEGATIVE SPIRIT `DWELLING' HATE DRIVEN M-I-N-D;
IS THE DEVIL'S (WORKSHOP)!!! # HASH TAG, SNAP OUT
OF IT. - TRANSFIGURATIVELY - NOWHERE TO MR.HYDE'
'RIGHT 'DR. JEKYLL.❞
'WHEREAS THIS HERE BEING A GAME WINNING 'MINDFUL INTERCEPTION
OF A POTENTIAL EVIL DOERS ONSLAUGHT...
REVITALIZING NEW-AGE 'SET YOU STRAIGHT' CURRICULUM ANYONE?

WANTED
New leader, new nation, new world
'READ HIM AND WEEP'

ONE CENT
WE NEED YOU!

THE ADVENTURE BEGINS HERE.

"Open Season on Common Folk Citizens"
Another episode of ... Again!

'POLICE STATE' TAX PAYERS! - THAT 'THIS DOCTOR, WILL SEE YOU NOW!!!

(((END OF DAZE ON BORROWED TIME)))

" The Shots Still Echo".
The truth about mass shootings

'REMINISCENT OF ALL THOSE FORCE FED, PAST
AND PRESENT, HORRIFIC CRIMINALS OUT THERE;
THAT 'NEVER DIGESTED' THE 'JESUS BAIT!!!

- NOR DID ANY OF THOSE 'PEDOPHILIA CLERGY; OR BOY SCOUT BUCKOOS; ALONG WITH THE MILITARY DEVIATE.

REMEMBERING **those who didn't make it home.**
Americans wonder: Where can I be safe?
`Resistance must be heard´

CONNECTICUT SCHOOL MASSACRE DECEMBER 14, 2012 "President Obama,
What we have not seen is leadership: not from the White House and not from Congress.
That must end today. This is a national tragedy and it demands a national response."

SHOW ME THE Democracy !!! SHOW ME THE Democracy !!!

BRING IT ON ANSWERS TO 'IT'S THE CURRICLUM STUPID'.

'MENTAL HEALTH-CARE VIA 'POSITIVE INFLUENCE' SAVES LIVES;

'YOURS TRULY, THE BEST ON THE PLANET AT DISHING THIS OUT IN VOLUMES...

Imagemakers "stop this cover-up!"

ENTER CLASSROOM SAVIOR OF THE WORLD

RIGHT FROM WRONG, GOOD FROM EVIL, ON RELIGION? GIVE ME 'ALL YOUR FLUNKIES! YOU DON'T NEED
A WAFER COMMUNION TO BE IN SYNC WITH THIS CRACKER. A MAN HAS GOT TO KNOW 'HIS SAME PAGE
RELIGIOUS LIMITATIONS, OR THE WHOLE WORLD JUST ALL BECOMES A 'GO TO HELL SOCIETY! - AS
LIKE IN AL-QAIDA'S 'DOGMA, IT'S ALL JUST FOAMING AT THE MOUTH...

TO ALL MY RELIGIOUS COMPETITORS "WHEN YOUR DOGMA QUITS BARKING
FREEDOM OF CHOICE' IS FOR YOU TO PREACH 'MY GOSPEL AND KEEP ALL YOUR
$$$ PARISHIONERS. OR SUFFER THE CONSEQUENCES OF HEAVY DUTY COMPETITION.

POINT BLANK

YOURS TRULY, BOOK PROPOSAL WRITTEN IN (1999) DURING THE
COLUMBINE TRAGEDY. DYLAN KLEBOLD'S RECORDED FAREWELL
CRUEL WORLD FINAL STATEMENT. CONFIDENT SELF-ASSURED 'EXCUSE!'
""I KNOW I'M GOING TO A BETTER PLACE THAN HERE""

"NOT ON MY WATCH YOU SPECULATING REPULSIVE PUNK; **Refresher Course Revisited.** ⇾

WELCOME TO **The** formation of a conscience;
"**My** opinion will change how people think and behave."

Searching For 'Real Closure?

'ON A MISSION FROM GODZILLA; WAKE-UP CALL, ACTION-STOPPER.

"I BELIEVE YOU CAN MAKE PEOPLE NICE.'

enough to support the brain.

THIS HERE BEING A HOW TO GUIDE!   YOURS TRULY, 1999

"TERRORIST" <u>MASS MURDERERS</u>, SERIAL KILLERS, ETC; 'DETERRENT PROPOSAL'
EXAMPLE: ORLANDO, FRANCE, TEX CHURCH, CHRIST CHURCH, PARKLAND, LAS VEGAS, ELPASO, ETC.!

The Horrors of BUSINESS AS USUAL TERRORISM.

"Open Season on Common Folk Citizens"

'SOMEONE MUST STAND UP TO OUR CLUELESS APOLOGETICAL GOVERNMENT; THEY
CAN'T PROTECT US' (VS) THESE WARP MINDED DESPICABLES! THEREFORE, =

WE'RE NOT GONNA TAKE IT ANYMORE BEGINS HERE!

TODAY'S BRIEFING "DETERRENT PROPOSAL"

PROMO <u>EXAMPLE</u> AN '<u>ALL-FAITHS</u>' **mecca** FACING WEST

MULTI-BILLION DOLLAR,

'<u>TOURISM PILGRIMAGE</u>'

'NO PLACE LIKE HELL' <u>SATANIC BURIAL GROUND</u>,

(((D.N.A. "ETC" - OR NOT.)))

'SPIT ON YOUR GRAVE' REALISTIC CLOSURE,

<u>HORRIFIC CRIME</u>,

—— C-O-N-S-E-Q-U-E N-C-E-S ——

"<u>DETERRENT PROPOSAL</u>"

"MOCKED FOR ETERNITY"

'JUST A REMINDER "THY WILL" BE DONE ON EARTH, AS IT IS IN 'HELL.

'YOUR INFAMOUS NAME WRITTEN IN STONE FOR SERVICES RENDERED TO SATAN.
(((WITH A RECURRING 'MAKE YOUR DAY' CELEBRATORY <u>HELL</u> ACCOMMODATIONS RITUAL.)))

'<u>HELL</u> "IF YOU BUILD THIS THEY WILL COME" <u>HELL</u>'

JUST NORTH OF RENO, NV. OFF 395.

- A DAILY VISITING FIELD-DAY,.

'WE WILL OFFICIALLY BURY YOU' PROJECT EXTRAVAGANZA.

—— TO MAKE'UM THINK, IS TO MAKE'UM BLINK! ====

" we Can prevent tragedy."

(65)

'RIGHTEOUSLY COMBATING MADNESS'

'YOUR CALL'

INTELLEGIENCE (VS) PROPERTY DEVASTATION "ETC"

'STOP THE MOB MENTALITY MAYHEM;

AND GET THE SCHOOLING YOU'VE BEEN DENIED!!!

'BULLY MACHOISM KILLED ERIC, BULLY MACHOISM KILLED GEORGE...

Tell It Like It Is
READING REVOLUTION
"Storytelling on a grand scale"

- OR JUST ANOTHER EPISODE OF 'END OF DAZE ON BORROWED TIME' THE GEORGE FLOYD TRAGEDY!
THUS ALL BOILS DOWN TO ' IT'S THE CURRICULUM STUPID ' EVERYONE CAN BITCH AND MOAN
ABOUT THIS STORY, 'UNTILL YOU COME ACROSS WITH A YOURS TRULY, THE RIGHT BITCHER AND
MOANER,'OR NOTHINGS EVER GOING TO CHANGE. WHEREAS, I'VE BEEN IN DEMOCRACY PRISON FOR
FAR TO LONG! THE POLICE FORCE (VS) THEIR OWN INSIDER MACHO FORCE'. 'I'M A MAN, I'VE
DEALT WITH BEING CONFRONTED WITH THE MENTALITY OF 'STREET PEOPLE JUST LIKE THIS; "IT'S
A GUY THING"!!! 'THE HIRING OF POLICE OFFICERS HAS GOT TO CHANGE TO I.Q. CITY. THE
'FIRST "I CAN'T BREATH STAND-OFF" WAS A PERFECT EXAMPLE OF THE 'MACHO POLICE FORCE IN
ACTION. BASED ON THE 'SEVERITY OF THE CRIME'?! ACTION LIKE THIS SHOULD HAVE NEVER
TAKEN PLACE. LET THIS BE A STANDARDIZATION. THEY GAVE IT THE 'YOU PUSHED MY MOTHER
IN FRONT OF A TRACTOR TRAILER TO FACE HER DEATH ROUTINE!!! 'THESE STORIES SHOULD
HAVE NEVER BEEN WRITTEN... I FEEL SORRY FOR THE POLICE OFFICERS THAT THIS HOLDS A
REFLECTION ON. I FEEL SORRY FOR THE YOUNG BLACK BAR OWNER THAT LOST EVERYTHING. HAD
I LIVED THERE I MIGHT HAVE BEEN ONE OF HIS CUSTOMERS - IN BRIEF. 'AS FOR THE REST OF
THIS TRAINING PROGRAM' "READ MY BOOK, PUBLISHING SOON 6/20"
'THE CHRONICLES OF DR. SUNDAY'...

AMERICAN WRITERS INSTITUTE PROUDLY PRESENTS
journalist Release of
C H R O N I C L E S
Freedom at Work - DO SOMETHING ABOUT IT -
future is no Kidding matter.
first steps into democracy
RIGHT ON TRACK

65 1/2

one for the books
"TEACHING INTELLIGENCE"
Review of reviews:

← IN REFERENCE TO HATE CRIMES →

IN QUESTION THE CASE OF S.CAROLINA, CHURCH MASS MURDERER,'DYLANN ROOF'
"ETC". LACKING "THIS" EDUCATION, HE WAS A 'UN-CHALLENGED'
FREE-RANGE NARROW MINDED RACIST...
- AS WAS ANTISMITIC FLORIDA SCHOOL SHOOTER; ALONG WITH MEXICAN RACIST, ELPASO SHOOTER.

'A MENTAL HEALTH CARE, OBLIGATORY 'TEACHABLE MOMENT;
'ON A MISSION FROM GODZILLA; WAKE-UP CALL, ACTION-STOPPER!!!
EDUCATIONALLY SPEAKING, INTRODUCING, FAITH BASED INITIATIVES FINEST HOUR!
FIRST AND FOREMOST 'THE PRIORITY OF EDUCATION' IS THAT OF BEING A MORALLY
PRINCIPLED ONE. ♫ I WANT YOU TO SHOW ME THE WAY - EVERYDAY!!!

BACK-TO-SCHOOL WITH RACIST 'LITERARY' EXORCISM CLASS 101 ...
(((Vintage Journalism)))
When words need to be said COMMON CORE PROPOSAL

TEACHING INTELLIGENCE, "SPOTLIGHT ON RACISM"

THE CLEAR THINKING COMMON GROUND OF ONE'S HAVING
INTELLIGENCE, IS SITUATIONALLY BEING ABLE TO
ACKNOWLEDGE, OR DETECT --- EXAMPLE: GOOD COP, BAD COP;
GOOD WHITE MAN, BAD WHITE MAN; GOOD BLACK MAN, BAD BLACK MAN;
GOOD PIT-BULL, BAD PIT-BULL; ETC, ETC, ETC. A TEACHABLE MOMENT?
IN RETROSPECT, - HOW TO BREAK-UP ONE'S 'NEGATIVE CONGLOMERATORY THOUGHTS IN
THE JUDGEMENT OF OTHERS! SIGNED: THE DEVIL'S WORST NIGHTMARE... AUTHOR'S NOTE:
"DEROGATORY NAME CALLING BY WAY OF LEADERSHIP; CAN GIVE ROOT TO THE WAY OF ONE'S
VIEWING OF OTHERS".   'TELLING IT LIKE IT IS.

= IN TESTIMONY WHEREOF = THIS IS ONE'S 'POSITIVE' BRAIN ON REPEAT DIALING!
WHEREAS TO FIND 'POSITIVE SAMENESS' WITHIN YOUR FELLOW MAN 'IS TO FIND HEAVEN
ON EARTH' S-A-N-E-N-E-S-S = AMEN.

'MIRACLE OF UNDERSTANDING'?! " MEDIA BANNED
Atrocities of Democracy, WE THE PEOPLE COVER up."

"FREEDOM OF EXPRESSION REFERS NOT JUST TO THE
MEDIA BUT ALSO TO THE FREEDOM OF ALL CITIZENS'
FREEDOM TO THINK, SPEAK, WRITE AND EXPRESS
THEMSELVES WITHOUT GOVERMENT RETALIATION. IT
PROTECTS THE RIGHT OF 'MINORITIES TO BE HEARD
AND PROMOTES CREATIVITY, OF NEW IDEAS AND
SOLUTIONS THAT CAN BENEFIT THE NATION".

(66)

Sustained conversation on race
'This Is a Major'
PAGE 66, AND THEN SOME.
miracle GOT GOD? Protest'

A WAKE-UP CALL!

– THUS A NATIONWIDE 'HOLIDAY TRADITION OF BIG CITY, SHOOT-UM-UP.

FINALLY... LIFE INSURANCE
–YOU CAN AFFORD–

Love thy Neighbor GOD.

'Great lessons in protests'

Truth Seminar Series

Reality Check ✳

JULY 4TH, 2020 "STOP THE INSANITY"
ONE 'EXAMPLE' CHICAGO, 17 PEOPLE SHOT AND KILLED; 80 PEOPLE SHOT.
– ELSEWHERE IN U.S.A. ON THAT DAY, OTHER NIGHTMARISH STORIES...
'BLACK ON BLACK' CRIME; SHOOT-UM-UP.'GET REAL
✳ 'BLACK LIVES MATTER' STARTS AT HOME... SIGNED: SOMEONE

WHO BOUGHT IN AND GIVES A DAMN...
THEREFORE, AS IS STORY IN RETROSPECT;
IN TRYING TO CONVINCE PEOPLE THAT CURE-ALL 'BLACK LIVES MATTER' TO A
RUN-OF-THE-MILL RACIST; IS LIKE TRYING TO CONVINCE TRUMP, INTO VOTING FOR BIDEN...

Time Out! When words need to be said.

"TREATED AS IF THEY WERE = NONE OF THOSE PEOPLE THAT WERE KILLED ON JULY 4th,
WERE EXPENDABLE!!! – TALK ABOUT INJUSTICE; 'ALL THOSE INNOCENT PEOPLE ARE
'ALSO WORTHY OF A PROTEST SANITY MARCH"!!! OR, MOTHERS AGAINST THE MOTHERS
THAT KILLED THEM. (EXAMPLE) THE YOUNG MAN FROM CHICAGO, WHO WAS GROWING UP
TO BECOME AN ALL WORLD FOOTBALL PLAYER. ⧸ THE JOHN LEWIS TYPE KID, FROM
OAKLAND THAT WANTED TO GROW-UP AND CONTRIBUTE TO THE BETTERMENT OF SOCIETY.
⧸⧸ CONCLUSIVELY: "GOD IN ONE'S LIFE IS THE ANSWERE". 'PROTEST MARCH THIS!!!
FOLLOW-UP ON PAGE 69...

`And They All Lived Happily Ever After.

Writer never backed down.

DUMB (VS) DUMBER

defining mission a must read
SOME OF THE BRIGHTEST LEGAL MINDS
NEVER WENT TO LAW SCHOOL.

HIGHER SPIRITUALITY! - IT'S NICE TO BE THE 'GOD LOVE ME' SMARTEST
ONE ON THE PLANET, PLAN IT; AND 'NOBODY SOUGHT OUT MY OPINION ABOUT
THE RECENT ATLANTA COP KILLING. 'THE SUSPECT SHOULD HAVE WENT FOR THE
(EVIDENCE) BREATHE'ALIZER AS OPPOSED TO THE STUN'GUN; REALIZING THAT
THIS IS WHAT WILL EVENTUALLY CATCH UP TO HIM! - HISTORY REPEATS ITSELF'
'WHY IS IT THAT I SEEM TO BE THE ONLY ONE THAT EVER SAW THIS 'MOVIE
BEFORE?! S. CAROLINA, WHERE THE WHITE COP, SHOOTS THE BLACK GUY RUNNING
AWAY IN THE BACK KILLING HIM; AND GETTING LIFE IN PRISON!!! "POLICE REFORM,
NEW COP TRAINING PROGRAM SCENARIO; IS WHERE YOU SHOOT THE LEGS OUT FROM
UNDER THE SUSPECT; AND YOU GET TO EAT AT WENDY'S ON A REGULAR BASIS FOR
THE REST OF YOUR LIFE"... IN CONCLUSION: 'REFORMATION MATTERS' "SEEING
HOW GEORGE WASHINGTON, ONCE OWNED SLAVES; JUST SEND ME 'ALL OF YOUR ONE
DOLLAR BILLS, AND I'LL DISPOSE OF THEM PROPERLY"...

"YOURS TRULY, VINTAGE JOURNALISM, NATIONWIDE, LETTERS TO THE EDITOR".
- "AND 'NOT ONE OF THEM, PUBLISHED 'MY POINT OF VIEW". 'STOP THE WORLD, I WANT TO GET ON!!!

NOBODY ASKED ME BUT *Looking Back*

HAD JOHNNIE COCHRAN, BEEN THE INITIAL PROSECUTING ATTORNEY
IN THE RODNEY KING TRIAL!!!

~~Los Angeles rioting~~

SinSinnati RioTiNG, APRIL 2001 POINT OF EMPHASIS

"NATIONWIDE! THEY NEED TO HIRE MORE BLACK POLICE OFFICERS,
TO PATROL BLACK COMMUNITIES"...

NO'
"THIS HERE BEING A REALISTIC 'HOW TO'

GUIDE IN DE'FUNDING THE POLICE DEPARTMENT"...

"ANARCHIES FINEST HOUR"

LIVING IN A SOCIETY WHERE THE BEST WAY TO GET BACK AT AND
UN-EMPLOY ALL THOSE RUTHLESS POLICE OFFICERS, ALONG WITH ALL
THE HIGHFALUTIN' PEOPLE WORKING IN THE COURT SYSTEM, IS TO
'B-E-H-A-V-E = Y-O-U-R-S-E-L-F' AND THAT'LL HURT'EM OHO SO
BIG TIME IN THEIR POCKET BOOKS; ARE YOU G-A-M-E EVERYONE???

"EXPERIENCE HAVING A BEAUTIFUL MIND".

'THIS IS OUR '1ST RODEO!!!

American dream
protesting racial inequality
'Learn*ing* from history,'
THANKS FOR
THE MEMORIES
WE'RE HERE FOR THE LONG HAUL
For the greater good
'freedom' needs me'.
Just the Facts ...

JUST WHEN 'YOU THOUGHT YOU' HAD HEARD 'ALL THE RACIALLY CHARGED
GRIEVANCES, THAT COULD POSSIBLE BE OUT THERE; ALONG COMES THE
HISPANIC, LATINO CONTINGENCY, POPING UP RIGHT OUT OF THE TORTILLA
FACTORIES!!! - VIA AN OVER-ALL NATIONWIDE 'WHOLE ENCHILADA PERCENTAGE
OF THE POPULATION; THIS HERE BEING A VALAD INDICATOR OF THIS HERE
A 'MAJOR INJUSTICE. "IN BRIEF EXAMPLES JUST TO NAME A FEW" - AS FAR AS

HAVING A 'HOME-BOY HISPANIC IN NASCAR = 0.   'SATURDAY NIGHT LIVE
REGULARS; = 0. PRO-HOCKEY PLAYERS; = 0. ETC. IN WATCHING THE ACADEMY
AWARDS OVER THE YEARS; ALL THE KITCHEN HELP BUT 'NO' CONTESTANTS! 'OR
MAYBE JAY-LO, WHO'S LIKE OUR TOKEN 'DON'T ROCK THE BOAT' REPRESENTATION.
TV$ COMMERICAL POPULATION % WISE JUSTICE??? "SPOT ON I LOVE AND RESPECT$,
ALL OF THE BLACK POPULATIONS ASSERTIVENESS TOWARDS 'ALL THESE ENTITIES,
ETC. - "BUT FOR ONE' EXAMPLE. 'I NEVER SAW ANYTHING DEROGATORY ABOUT
UNCLE BEN'S PICTURED RICE! - GIVE CREDIT TO THERE BEING ALOT OF GREAT
BLACK COOKS. 'TO ME' THIS IS FIRST CLASS QUALITY RICE, AND THE BEST IN
THE BUSINESS. THEREFORE, 'GIVE IT UP! 'INTRINSICALLY, STOOP LABOR NOMORE'
     - PUT MY HISPANIC FACE ON THAT RICE PROMOTION... ☺

The damaging existence of racism :
Writer never backed down.

"Open Season on Common Folk Citizens"

NEWS OF RECORD on **Gunman** GONE WILD,

'ORLANDO NIGHTCLUB GUNMAN'S PRIORITIZED MOTIVE?!

HISTORY ON DISPLAY ANALYSIS 6/16

((('AS WE LEARN IN 'DUDEWILLRATONME' SCRIPTURE,)))

THE GOSPEL ACCORDING TO A *Call Time Out!*

VERIFICATION ACCURACY ANSWERS TO: QURAN/BIBLE,

WHEN A RELIGION ENDORSES 'NEGATIVITY ON SUCHAS

'LGBT HOMOPHOBIA' ALONG WITH THE SUBJUGATION OF WOMEN IS A

CASTING PROGRAMER SPECIAL EFFECTS 'WRITTEN BY MAN, INSPIRED BY THE DEVIL.

MAY--DAY **Time to Rescue** RELIGION; *Humans need to evolve.*

" ALL THIS 'HAS GOT TO BECOME' YESTERDAYS PRAYER BOOK!!! "

((("WHAT STARTED WITH RELIGION CAN ONLY BE RECTIFIED BY RELIGION".)))

♫ COME TOGETHER RIGHT NOW, OVER ME. ' SIGNED: SAVIOR OUT OF THE 'BULL' PEN.

Religious 'extremists'. Or 'REALISTIC POSSIBILITY ABOUT =FREQUENT FLYER=

'ORLANDO NIGHTCLUB GUNMAN'S PRIORITIZED MOTIVE?!

I BELIEVE THE 'REAL STORY' BEHIND THE STORY' WAS THAT

'THIS' WAS A 'GAY GUY' MISFIT WITH A MONSTER PERSONALITY;

THAT COULDN'T FIND ANYBODY WANTING TO DANCE SHEIK

TO SHEIK WITH HIM. FRUSTRATED AND HAVING AN EFFETE FEELING

OF BEING A MATEENE WIENIE WITHIN THE 'IN CROWD'. 'SEXUALLY

UN-FULFILLED HE REVENGEFULLY TOOK OUT ALL OF HIS FRUSTRATIONS

OUT ON THE CLUB'S PATRONS!

Americans wonder: Where can I be safe?

IS NIGHTCLUB MASSACRE KILLING THE NEW NORM; ALONG WITH A JIHADI

DRIVERS ED; CRASH COURSE IN USING REAL DUMMIES WITH A 'INVALID'

LICENSE TO KILL??? **Vintage Journalism**; "END OF DAZE ON BORROWED TIME; 'POLICE

STATE" THAT EVERYTIME 'POSITIVE SUGGESTION GET'S TOSSED OUT

"SUCH AS THIS **'NATIONWIDE LETTERS TO THE EDITOR'**

NEGATIVITY, WILL ALWAYS BE THERE TO FILL IN THE GAP.

What's News ! QURAN/BIBLE, revision Caveman

Extremists **Smoke and Mirrors Roll Over**

Convention , CLEARANCE SALE.

Man's explosive frustration

THANK YOU JESUS!
JUST ANOTHER THORN IN THA SIDE OF
YOUR MINISTRY'S IMPACT ON SOCIETY ETC; OR
EVERYONE LIVING IN LOS ANGELES, NEEDS ICE WATER.

'BEER SUMMIT MULTITASKING ON MY DOWNTIME WITH'

THIS THING CALLED PRAYER

A CLASSIC CONFERENCE with **BIG TEASER**

PRAYING COMPLAINING CONCEPTUALLY AT HOME
WHILE SCARFING DOWN A BEER AND THUMBING
THROUGH THA RADIO STATIONS TRYING TO FIND A
SONG I LIKE 'OR IT'S LIKE THIS

GOD,

ONLY 3 DAYS OFF IN THA LAST 65,
BETWEEN WORKING MY DON'T QUIT
MY DAY JOB, AND WRITTING THIS BOOK.,
I'VE EITHER WORKED 16 OR 18 HOUR
DAYS, SOMETIMES ROLLING THA CLOCK
WITHOUT ANY SLEEP! FOR WHAT I ASK?
'FOR WHAT? STILL THUMBING AROUND RADIO
STATIONS I PAUSE TO HEAR A THAUMATURGIC
CONSOLING VOICE SPEAKING OUT FROM THA RADIO!

Cloud Nine 'Response FROM THE TOP

"I NEVER GET A VACATION."

(68)

NEWS YOU CAN USE
2018

' Vintage Journalism stories '

'RIGHTEOUSLY COMBATING MADNESS'
Murder, gunfire grow in Chicago

E
T
C.

DEVIL DAMN-IT, WITH ALL THIS GHETTO STYLE KILLING THAT'S BEEN GOING ON IN CHICAGO!
IF YOU CAN EXCEL IN BASKETBALL, EXCEL IN FOOTBALL, 'YOU NEED TO EXCEL IN THE GAME
OF SOUL'S IN RELIGION! 'ORGANIZE'. IT TAKES A "POSITIVE" VILLAGE TO RAISE A CHILD.
THIS ALL STEMS FROM THE LACK OF 'NOT HAVING A PREDOMINANT "GOD CONSCIOUS ENVIRONMENT"
'THE DEVIL IS ROOSTING THERE' IN AS FAR AS TEAM 'SPIRIT' RELIGION GOES; YOU GUYS ARE
THE LAST PLACE IN THE NATION TO RAISE A FAMILY. I RECALL WHEN I WAS A YOUNG MAN GROWING
UP 'THERE JUST DOWN THE STREET; I WAS A TAVERN LEAGUE SOFTBALL PLAYER AND MANAGER WITH
AN ALL WHITE TEAM I HAD GROWN UP WITH; PLAYING IN A PICK-UP FRIENDLY GAME AGAINST AN
ALL BLACK TEAM JUST UP THE STREET, OR INNER CITY GUYS! JUST THE SAME PRIDE (VS) PRIDE;
IN AS FAR AS OVER-ALL ATHLETICISM GOES, WE WERE OUT NUMBERED BIG TIME, AND IT DIDN'T
LOOK GOOD FOR A BUNCH OF CRACKERS RUNNING AROUND LIKE THEY WERE ALL PLAYING WITH PIANOS
STRAPPED TO THEIR BACKS. TORTOISE (VS) HARE, HERE WE GO!- AS THE STORY GOES BECAUSE OF
   OUR FLAWLESS FUNDAMENTAL SKILLS; ERRORLESS WE PUT ON A HARD FAUGHT CLINIC AND WALKED
AWAY WITH A TWO RUN VICTORY! MORAL OF THE STORY; 'TILL YOU CAN PROVE TO ME, FROM MY
PERSPECTIVE THAT THRU ORGANIZATIONAL SKILLS THAT 'YOU CAN RID THE DEVIL FROM THE HOOD!
'AND IF YOU CAN'T - I'LL ALWAYS BELIEVE THAT CRACKERS ARE THE BETTER ATHLETE'S...
     GAME ON BROTHER MAN ??? MAKE IT SO THAT WHITEY WANT'S TO MOVE BACK IN !!! :)

'TAKE THE BIG CHALLENGE'

- AND RID THE NEIGHBORHOOD OF 'THE CURSE OF THE 'IN-SALTINE CRACKER'...

'SURRENDERING' INFORMATION. "QUOTE" **HOROSCOPE Libra.**

A lot of people won't even realize the truth of the situation until you point it out. 👉

Tell me more TIME CAPSULE.

IN PART AUTHOR'S CREDENTIALS: CHICAGO SUBURBS '1960'. -AS A STEP-BACK
SCEPTICAL CATHOLIC, GRADE SCHOOL GRADUATE, I RECALL BEING BACK IN
7th GRADE WITH A HANDFUL OF OTHER KIDS ON THE PLAYGROUND AND IN A
PLAYFUL MOMENT WITH A COUPLE OF NUNS THAT WE CONFRUNTED AND ASKED
THEM THE QUESTION. 'WHAT DO YOU GUYS KNOW IF ANYTHING ABOUT THE
FUTURE OF OUR SOCIETY? - AND THEIR RESPONSE TO US WAS, THAT IN
'1980' SOMETHING IS GOING TO HAPPEN THAT'S 'EVENTUALLY'
GOING TO CHANGE THE WORLD FOR THE BETTER!
FASTFORWARD '1980' ENTER THE GRASS ROOTS
REVOLUTIONARY FOUNDATION OF THIS AUTHOR'S RELIGION...

SUNDAY, NOVEMBER 7, 1999 # Pope challenges to promote

Catholicism, *"STATES THAT EVERYONE SHOULD HAVE THA RIGHT TO PROMOTE ONE'S OWN RELIGIOUS BELIEFS!"*

Attention WALmart Shoppers *"Now* **OPEN"** (69)

CONNECTICUT SCHOOL MASSACRE DECEMBER 14, 2012 "President Obama,
What we have not seen is leadership: not from the White House and not from Congress.
That must end today. This is a national tragedy and it demands a national response."

☞ **OK!** BRING IT ON ANSWERS TO

SHOW ME THE Democracy !!! SHOW ME THE Democracy !!!

Heard Any Good 'SHOW STOPPER' Sermons Lately?

TAKING AWAY ONE'S EVIL EXCUSES, 'BREAK ON THRU TO THE OTHERSIDE'

ANALYSIS 'VERSUS' PARALYSIS : 'FUNCTIONALLY

IN BRIEF: LAWYERS ON GIVING THEIR MOST LIKELY EXCUSE RESPONSE FOR 'HOLMES AND LANZA, ETC.
YOUR HONOR, OUR CLIENT IS FUNCTIONALLY INSAIN! PREMEDITATEDLY, HE DROVE OVER THERE TO THE
CRIME SCENE MUCH MORE STABLE THAN 'MOST SO CALLED SAIN PEOPLE COULD, AND COMMITTED THAT
-A-C-T-.

BRAIN SCIENTISTS HAVEN'T PINNED DOWN WHY SOME ' PEOPLE ACT ON THE FEELING

IS THERE A PSYCHOLOGY OF HATE WE NEED TO UNDERSTAND BETTER?

"Haters like company — it makes them feel better."

♫ WORKING ON MYSTERYS WITHOUT ANY CLUES???
TO NO AVAIL COLO. MOVIE MASSACRE JOKER, WAS 'SOUL'
SEARCHING FOR, 'SNAP OUT OF IT' AVOIRDUPOIS TRUTH!
THEREFORE INTRODUCING VINTAGE YOURS TRULY,
REVITALIZING NEW-AGE 'SET YOU STRAIGHT' CURRICULUM
ANYONE???

RECALCITRANT TO SOCIETY, THESE MONSTERS WERE ALL
CREATED RIGHT BEFORE OUR VERY OWN EYES!
THEREFORE ENTER SYLLABUS DIFFERENCE MAKER,
DR. NOMORE DUCKANDCOVER.

"WHEREAS TO KNOW ONE'S WORKABLE MIND, IS TO
BLOW ONE'S MIND; TILL THEY GET YOURS TRULY, TRUTH
SERUM MENTALLY OVERHAULED, NOTHINGS GOING TO CHANGE.
IMMUNE TO UN-IMPACTIVE NEANDERTHAL RELIGIONS DILLY,
DALLY, DOGMA! 'EVIL MINDED CLOSET ATHEISTS' ARE
NOTHING MORE THEN REAL LIFE FOCUSED ZOMBIES
ON A MISSION FROM godZILLA...
♫ TRY TO DETECT IT; IT'S NOT TO LATE! (70)

In your Face book
READY FOR PRIME TIME
Man in video cites rejection, blames women
Calif. murder suspect had manifesto of rampage

"I didn't want it to come to this," Rodger said. "I desperately wanted a way out."

"QUOTE NEWS PRINT HEAD-LINE SET-UP"/ WITH STORY RESPONSE FOLLOW-UP BY YOURS TRULY.
(SEXUAL HEALING) "WELCOME TO THE 'END' OF SWEEPING HUMAN SEXUALITY UNDER
THE RUG" • 'RX' WHEREBY THIS HERE BEING 'SHOCK THERAPY' TO THE SO-CALLED
GOODY TWO SHOES IMAGE CONSCIOUS, NATIONWIDE STRAIT JACKET ASSOCIATION, ETC. ETC.

KNIVES, AND GUNS, AND A VEHICLE, OH' MY; THIS GUY RODGER
SHOULD HAVE BEEN 'LITERALLY DIAGNOSED AS ONE HORNY DEVIL!
BY WAY OF HIS CRYING OUT FOR HELP VIDEO AND MANIFESTO, IS
ALL EVIDENCE TO THAT. THEREFORE, ENTER YOURS TRULY, HISTOR
-ICALLY THE MOST GIFTED SHRINK THAT'S EVER WRITTEN A 'RX'.
ALL HE NEEDED TO DO TO RECYCLE HIS MINDSET AND FUNCTION
NORMALLY, WAS TO HAVE SPENT THAT WEEKEND AT A 'WHORE HOUSE;
AND BY MONDAY EVENING THE NEW MISTER DYNAMIC PERSONALITY,
WOULD HAVE PROBABLY BEEN OUT DOING STAND -UP COMEDY!

"INTRODUCING 'COUGAR CITY' EPOCHAL PROPOSAL"

♫ MONEY AIN'T FOR NOTHING, AND THE COUGARS ARE ALL FREE.
'WHERE BOY MEETS PEARL' WHEREBY ONE WOMENS TRASH, IS ANOTHER WOMENS TREASURE!
50 SHADES OF BEING OVER 50, TO A COUGAR; GUYS IN THEIR 20'S ARE PRICELESS.
'IF YOU BUILD THIS THEY WILL COME'.

Time to reach the next level of

HARMONY? - "I'D EVEN GO AS FAR AS HAVING A $20 DOLLAR,
PLAIN JANE, HORNY WOMENS WHORE HOUSE; THUS ACTION FOR EVERYBODY HORNY.

'Time has come' for Invention of the Year

"LEGALIZE 'CONSENTING' NO STRINGS ATTACHED PROSTITUTION" ESPECIALLY
IN THE ='VACINITY'= OF COLLAGE AND MILITARY INSTATUTIONS. WITH ALL THE
THANK YOU FOR YOUR SERVICE, OPEN SEASON' MILITARY MALE SEX OFFENDERS OUT
THERE, ALONG WITH ALL THE 'INTOLORABLE' ONE IN FIVE COLLEGE YOUNG WOMEN
BEING SEXUALLY ASSULTED!!! YEARS AGO I SENT THIS SAME INFO,
OUT. TO THE NATIONWIDE MEDIA AND THEY NEVER WROTE BACK TO
THANK ME! IN REGARDS TO THIS CLONE CREEP, STORY OF
CHO-SEUNG-HUE KILL 32! HUE, WAS A HORNY DEVIL 'R-E-J-E-C-T'
REVENGEFUL EVIL DOER FROM A PICK AND CHOOSE ESCORT SERVICE
DENYING HIM SERVICE, AND THE REST IS ALL HISTORY. - IN
CONCERT WITH REVENGE, OR SUFFERING FROM BROKEN HEART SYNDROM,
JOKER HOLMS, WAS IN NEED OF SET YOU STRAIGHT 'RX' SEXUAL THERAPY.

Another episode of ...Again!

"OPEN SEASON ON COMMON FOLK CITIZENS"

"I CAN'T KEEP UP"!!!

" **The Shots Still Echo** "

"unforgettable images"

Tx Gunman fired point-blank at crying children in church, HISTORY ON DISPLAY.

OCT. 1ST 2017 " **Vegas shooter had lost money** "

WHAT YOU NEED TO KNOW

"PLUTOCRACY KILLS"

"THIS THING ABOUT THE LAS VEGAS SHOOTER; 'PROOF THEREOF' IN THE HISTORY OF PEOPLE 'EVER HAVING MEDIA ACCESS; 'NOBODY EVER IMPRESSED HIM ENOUGH TO HAVE CHANGED 'HIS CHOSEN END GAME OF EVENTS MIND". BIG GOT'CHA' - ANSWERS TO:

Atrocities of Democracy. "where to begin"

2012 FAITH FORUM *Do all religions offer a path to God?*

"THE GOOD NEWS MINE DOES 24/7 - 365,. THE BAD - DEMOCRACY DEPRIVED THIS ONE'S BEEN BIG TIME 'ROAD BLOCKED' FOR DECADES."

"Storytelling on a grand scale"

`showcases the truth

about what's happening behind the scenes 'WITH

A teachable moment' *wake-up call* Exhibit

'DETERRENT PROPOSAL'

"I BELIEVE YOU CAN MAKE PEOPLE NICE." (72)

Facing Down the Monster

LAS VEGAS THE SHOOTER: Stephen Paddock,

"RETIRED $$$ WAS A 64-YEAR-OLD WITH A TASTE FOR HIGH-STAKES POKER".
'PULLING STRINGS' AND KNOWING HIS 'STORED UP' FULL BLOWN TEMPER
TANTRUM, H-A-T-E FILLED MIND; YOU CAN 'BET' THE DEVIL LEAD HIM INTO
'EVERY CONSISTENT LOOSING SITUATION SO THAT HE COULD FINAL SOLUTION,
PULL THIS OFF"...

(TOM PETTY) SONG STATES ♪♫ EVEN LOSERS GET LUCKY ONCE IN A WHILE!

'RUMER HAS IT THAT HE WON LARGE FORTUNES; AND 'MORE SO' LOST LARGE FORTUNES;
CAUSING HIS NIGHTMARISH SCREAMING IN THE MIDDLE OF THE NIGHT! ♪♫ KNOW WHEN
TO HOLD'EM -ETC- KNOW WHEN TO RUN.

'MOTIVE OF SHOOTER'

$ LAS VEGAS / STILL PRETENDS THAT THEY HAVEN'T FIGURED OUT A MOTIVE YET"...

"R-E-A-D-I-N-G-B-E-T-W-E-E-N-T-H-E-L-I-N-E-S"

enough to support the brain

THE ADVENTURE BEGINS HERE

'PAY BACK' -FOR HIS PREDOMINATE GAMBLING LOSSES-
SIMPLY, A HATRED OF PEOPLE THAT KEPT BUILDING FROM HIS COMPOUNDED
GAMBLING FAILURES. 'THUS THE CREATION OF THIS HERE BEING A MONSTER MADE
IN THE U.S.A.

or

HATE DRIVEN CRAZY' IS ONLY HAVING TO 'SHRINK THE HATE PART. ☺

WHEREAS, MOST LIKELY 60% OF THE ROAD RAGE 'FLIP YOU OFF SOCIETY'
YOU SEE 'IN THIS HERE A GAMBLING TOWN'

"YOU CAN BET"

WAS BY SOMEBODY WHO JUST DROPPED A BUNDLE AT THE CASINO!

- AND THE OTHER 40% IS BY THE POOCH PUNT GUY

WHO'S GIRL'FRIEND JUST LEFT HIM FOR
A 'JOE COCKER SPANIEL...

—— FOR 'ALL THOSE YEARS OF HIS LIFE, BEFORE HE EVER MOVED TO A GAMBLING
COMMUNITY, HE WAS NOTHING MORE THAN A 'YOUR OK, I'M OK' INTROVERTED BORE...

Adding up the costs – Mystique no more!

'NOBODY SHOULD BE LEFT OUT OF TELLING
IT LIKE IT IS DEMOCRACY'

Treatment holds key to future
knowledge is your best commonsense •

(73)

'essential to formation of a conscience'

WELCOME TO The United States of Gambling.

Newsmakers, A RE-EDITED 1988 Editorial Democracy Prison Original, **Waiting to Exhale.** **2012** There's a good chance they're going to recognize him this year, Announcing **a new** "TRAIN YOUR BRAIN" COURSE OF STRATEGY **ON GAMING UNPREDICTABILITY!** **ARTICLES** **Refresher Course Revisited.** $ **Games** PEOPLE PLAY
SELF-IMPROVEMENT

Guidelines: Read, Listen and Win! IN GAMBLING, IT'S BETTER TO RECEIVE THAN GIVE! BETTING ON PIG SKINS OR PORK BELLIES, **PLAYED BY KINGS & COWBOYS.**, MANY A RELIGIOUS CONDEMNER OF GAMBLING HAVE LOST TONS OF MONEY IN THE STOCK MARKET., IN THAT ═══ YEARS LATER UP-DATE, SPOT ON! J-WALKING IN HEAVY TRAFFIC IS A RISKY GAMBLE., DRIVING WHILE USING A CELL-PHONE OR TEXTING WHILE DRIVING ETC, IS BIG TIME GAMBLING ETC. may 1988, **R I P P E D   F R O M   T H E   S K Y .** obey laws of God.

On Personal Money Management

a 'teachable moment'

"WINNING A CASINO JACK-POT IS LIKE GETTING A FREE CASH MONEY LOAN THAT VOLUNTARILY SOME PEOPLE WILL PAY BACK WITH ENTRUST.'

'JUST THE FACTS'

"CASINOS, ARE FUN AND EXCITING PLACES OF VENTURE FOR ANY RESPONSIBLE BILL PAYING ADULT, THAT KNOWS THE TRUE VALUE OF WHAT ONE CAN AFFORD TO WAGER' BEFORE MAKING A FOOL OF ONESELF.,

IN THAT EVERYTHING IN LIFE IS TO A DEGREE. WHEREAS THIS IS THE TYPE OF DISCIPLINE ONE MUST ACQUIRE TO WITHHOLD **A POSITIVE Self Esteem**?

:WARNING LABEL: 'FOR SOME; LOSING MONEY AT GAMBELING IS PAINFUL, AND CAN MAKE A M-O-N-S-T-E-R OUT OF YOU. "KEEP IN MIND, ALL THOSE PLUSH CASINOS YOU SEE, WERE BUILT ON GAMBLERS LOSINGS"...
YOURS TRULY, IN CONCLUSION TESTIMONY: 'GAMBLING IS AN INSULT TO MY INTELLIGENCE; - AND YET STILL 'ON OCCASION' I FIND MYSELF OUT THERE, FROM TIME TO TIME, GETTING INSULTED..(74)

The truth about mass shootings

OCT.1st = ROSEBURG, ORE. The gunman, Chris Mercer, 26,
2015 opened fire inside a classroom at Umpqua Community College.

Doctor's Shocking Revelation
'MOTIVE OF SHOOTER'

- BE NICE FOR 'CHRIST SAKE' WASN'T WORKING FOR THIS GUY! SHOOTING HIS
VICTIMS IN THE HEAD, HE WAS INTELLECTUALLY INSULTED BY THE DISNEYLAND
MENTALITY OF CHRISTIANITY. THEREFORE, WITH HIS FEELINGS OF BEING
MICKEY MOUSED' HE TOOK REVENGE ON HIS FELLOW STUDENTS. "HE CONSIDERED
HIMSELF TO BEING 'SPIRITUAL' AND YET SOMEHOW THE OVERBEARING 'NEGATIVE
SPIRIT' WITHIN HIMSELF TOOK OVER". 'PROFILE IN CONCLUSION' "HE WAS JUST
ANOTHER V-I-R-G-I-N / C-L-O-N-E OF CALIF; TERRORIZING HATEMUNGER ROGER'S
ETC, ETC, ETC"...

'REMINISCENT OF ALL THOSE FORCE FED, PAST
AND PRESENT, HORRIFIC CRIMINALS OUT THERE;
THAT 'NEVER DIGESTED' THE 'JESUS BAIT!!!
THEREFORE, I.Q. YOU IN ON THIS;
'GIVE IT UP FOR' YOURS TRULY, THE 'NEW WORLD ADAM'

Founder of 'THE POSITIVE Faith 'ONE WORLD' Religion.

SOME OF THE BRIGHTEST LEGAL MINDS NEVER WENT TO LAW SCHOOL.

CONCLUSIVE! DR.SUNDAY, (VERSUS) "THE DEVIL MADE ME DO IT! DEFENSE"...
NATIONWIDE LETTERS TO THE EDITOR; (1995) HEAD-TO-HEAD,
HERE'S THE SKINNY ON THE UNABOMBER 'NUTCRACKER' TRIAL.
IN REFERENCE TO 'HIS ACTIONS 'HE, WAS NOTHING MORE THEN
A MAD AT THE WORLD 'HARMFULLY CRAZY' INTROVERTED,
SELF-CENTERED TEED-OFF RECLUSE; SUCCUMBING TO 'ONE'S
OWN HATRED OR BITTERNESS. SURREALISTICALLY THE
'DEVIL' REACTING WITHIN THE DEFENDANTS OWN
NEGATIVE SUGGESTIVE HEINOUS SEED OF THOUGHT
SUB-CONSCIOUS; SUGGESTED TO HIM TO DO IT ===
AND 'HE THAT IS OF 'ONE'S OWN 'FREE WILL'
CHOSE TO DO 'CONSCIOUSLY AS SUCH!!!
NEW-AGE 'SET YOU STRAIGHT' CURRICULUM ANYONE?
ENCORE POINT BEING, YOU'D HAVE TO BE CRAZY
'NOT' TO PUBLICLY PRINT THIS MANIFESTO"... (75)

Psssst.

Want to know a secret?

THA PRISON SYSTEM IN THIS COUNTRY IS A TAX PAYER GOUGING $BIG BUSINESS!
(THA MORE LIFE IN PRISON HAND OUTS, THA $MERRIER·
'RIGHT DEATH PENALTY ABOLISHING, CALIF, GOV, NEWSOM! 'A VICTIMS OUTRAGE, PROVOCATOR...

Bringing To Life Tha Death Penalty yes !

Cost per day to punish: $80.25

Most of the 215,866 federal inmates in <u>2013</u> were there on drug charges. Average annual cost per inmate:

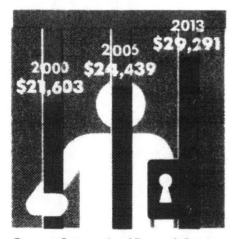

2013 $29,291
2005 $24,439
2000 $21,603

Sources Congressional Research Service; Bureau of Justice Statistics

Why it matters:

on Economic concerns:

CHECK THA MILEAGE.

REACH OUT AND SHOCK SOMEONE

'2020'

WHERE WE ARE NOW $?

aims to finding a solution !

WE'VE 'ALL' BEEN GIVEN A LIFE EXPECTANCY'
—— DEATH SENTENCE —— (76)

Tell me more TIME CAPSULE. ⟹

Presenting A Shaking tha Money Tree SOLUTION STOPPER.

'BY WAY OF ATLEAST WAREHOUSEING ALL THE HOMELESS, VIA THE FULFILLMENT OF 'BULK
CAPITAL PUNISHMENT, SHOWS HAVING A $JUSTIFIABLE PRINCIPLE! - THEREFORE BE IT
UNDERSTANDING, OR SOCIOLOGICAL MAYHEM. "WITNESS HOW DEMOCRACY WORKS IN ACTION"
'PROPOSAL OF' INDIVIDUALS, CHURCH GROUPS, OR ORGANIZATIONS, CAN NOW BUY ONE'S
LIFE SENTENCE VERSUS CAPITAL PUNISHMENT; AND ADOPT A HEINOUSTIC CRIMINAL IN A
INCARCERATED SETTING - BY WAY OF FUNDING THEIR ON GOING MEGA BUCKS EXTREMITY!
- ALTHOUGH THIS (WRITTEN IN 1983) VENTURE PACKAGE WILL 'NOT' BE TAX DEDUCTIBLE.
'INTRODUCING PETTIN PLACE. VISITATION RIGHTS BEYOND BELIEVE, OR SITTING ON THE
LAP OF YOUR FAVORIT MASS MURDER. PACIFISTICALLY SPEAKING, LOVE'UM AND LEAVE'UM
THERE TO ROT; THUS GIVING THEM A GUARANTEED $LIFE SENTENCE WITH ALL THE TRIMM-
INGS ; - KIND OF LIKE ALL THE 'TRIMMINGS THE HOMELESS PEOPLE JUST DREAM ABOUT...
'A SURPRISE IN EVERY KARMA; RIGHT GOV. NEWSOM'...

Activists 'bear witness' to PUBLIC AUCTION

(((SECRET - SAUCE - REVEALED)))

- ARE YOU AWARE THAT IN THE 'BIG' PICTURE OF LIFE, ONLY A TRUE
"PREDOMINANTLY POSITIVE SPIRIT FILLED, GOD LOVING, PROGRAMED PERSON"
'WOULD ONLY KILL IN SELF-DEFENSE, WAR OR JUSTIFIABLE CAPITAL PUNISHMENT $.

'WAKE UP AND SMELL THE C-O-P-Y'

America's Most Wanted:

((('PRAYER OF THA AFTER THA FACT SOCIETY')))

Vintage Journalism

Discover a New Dimension in Learning

IN TESTIMONY WHEREOF

GOD,

DIDN'T PUT US ON THIS HERE EARTH TO KILL ONE ANOTHER.
STATE OF MIND, FRAME OF MIND,
`NO STATE OF MIND IS PERMANENT!!!

'INSTIGATORS OF CRIME; STANDARDIZING OF ONE'S INTELLIGENCE'
(((CRIME PREVENTION)))

If you ignore -it,- it will go away.

"WHEREAS PATIENCE IS THA KEY!"

Lecturing FEATURES Take My Advice, Please (77)

reporter urges Pope to seek truth

FRIAR FLYER NEWSLETTERCOMMENTARY BY: THE NEW WORLD ADAM

What's behind criticism

Some friendly reminders:

- TAKING A FOLLOW ME LEADERSHIP STAND POPE FRANCIS, DECLARES HIS OPPOSITION
TO THE DEATH PENALTY! 'NICE GUYS FINISH LAST' WHEN IT COMES TO THE OVER-ALL
ECONOMIC QUALITY OF LIFE $BUDGET, FOR THE GREATER OF 'GOOD; HE'S PRAYER SC-
HOOL CLUELESS. 'FAKE NEWS' IS WHEN THEY TELL YOU IT COST MORE TO EXECUTE
THEM THAN IT DOES TO GIVE THEM TAX-PAYER MEGA BUCKS COMPOUNDED LIFE IN PRISON!
- A POCKET FULL OF POPULAR OPIOIDS AND A BON-FIRE, AND THEIR ALL GOOD TO GO!
'BIG BUSINESS' THE MORE THEY CAN HAND OUT LIFE LONG PRISON SENTENCES ANSWERS
TO, THE LONGER THEIR WELL PAYING JOBS GET THEM THRU THEIR RETIREMENT.
'JUST THE FACTS' LET ME BE THE FIRST TO INFORM YOU! "WE'VE ALL BEEN GIVEN
       A DEATH SENTENCE" WHEREAS THIS HERE IS NOTHING MORE THAN THE SHORT
CHANGING OF A IGNOMINIOUS ONE'S LIFE EXPECTANCY. TENACIOUSLY DOING UN - TO -
OTHERS; WHO WERE THE ORIGINAL INOVATORS OF 'THE CRUEL AND UNUSUAL PUNISHMENT'
EXTINGUISHER PROGRAM. - A HAUNTING 'EXAMPLE' TAKEN FROM VOLUMES; THE STORY
ABOUT A LOVING FATHER THAT COMES TO THE RESQUE OF HIS 16 YEAR OLD, DAUGHTER
WHO IS ABOUT TO BE RAPED BY A SERIAL KILLER WHO GUNS DOWN THE FATHER KILLING
HIM, THAN RAPES HIS DAUGHTER! - CARE TO CHANGE YOUR OPINION YET MR. POPE???
INCESSANTLY, WHY MUST THESE DEGENERATIVE LOW-LIFERS, HOLD PRIORITY OVER THE
NATIONWIDE UNFORTUNATE HOMELESS PEOPLE OUT THERE THAT WERE GIVEN 'THE DEATH
PENELTY' BY WAY OF THEIR FROZEN TUNDRA OVER-NIGHT ACCOMMODATIONS?...

In Testimony Whereof VICTIM'S OUTRAGE ●●●

'LETTUCE PREY, ACCORDING TO SLOW COOKER AL PASTOR;
'EXPERIENCE HAVING A BEAUTIFUL MIND'.

'*rhetoric of revolution* **IM PRUV ALL** '*Spiritual Awakening*'

A HIGH PRIORITIE OF THIS MAN'S RELIGION, FOCUSES ON
THOU SHELT NOT `INSTIGATE - KILL' FACTOR., - ARE YOU AWARE IN THE
'BIG' PICTURE OF LIFE THAT ONLY A TRUE "PREDOMINANTLY POSITIVE SPIRIT
FILLED, GOD LOVING, PROGRAMED PERSON" WOULD 'ONLY
KILL IN SELF-DEFENSE, (WAR) JUSTIFIABLE CAPITAL PUNISHMENT.
                        OR
((('PRAYER OF THE AFTER THE FACT SOCIETY')))

GOD, DIDN'T PUT US ON THIS HERE EARTH TO KILL ONE ANOTHER.,
STATE OF MIND, FRAME OF MIND, `NO STATE OF MIND IS PERMANENT!!!

If you ignore `it,' — it will go away

`(EXAMPLE) **"LEAD US NOT INTO TEMPATATION; BUT
DELIVER US FROM EVER' BECOMING EVIL' AMEN"**.

'RIGHT TO THE POINT'

LOOK AT YOUR RELIGION? NOW LOOK BACK AT MINE.

"WELCOME TO RELIGIOUS AND POLITICAL SUNDAY SCHOOL."

The end of silence?
NOVEMBER 2013
"New report on shooting in Newtown reaffirms WITH BULLYING issue Consistency

FRIEND'S COMMENTS

A friend of Nancy Lanza's, Marvin LaFontaine, said she was a devoted mother
to her two sons and that she showed up at Adam Lanza's elementary school
to protect him when he was picked on by other children.
when he was picked on by other children.
when he was picked on by other children. **"**

NEVADA - OCTOBER - 2013

IN REFERENCE TO THE SPARKS MIDDLE SCHOOL SHOOTING! - ONE CAN ONLY
'HARMLESSLY TEASE ANOTHER BY WAY OF HAVING A AMICABLE BOND WITH ONE
ANOTHER. WHEREAS IN 'THIS CASE, M-O-C-K-E-R-Y DRIVEN CAME TO SCHOOL
THAT DAY TOTING A GUN. = AND THE REST IS HISTORY.

AN AFTER SCHOOL SPECIAL MADE TO ORDER.

'A DEFINING TEACHABLE MOMENT'

CRIME PREVENTION?! (((HELLO))) KNOWLEDGE IS SAFETY:

"BULLY PREVENTION 'AWARENESS' CLINIC - YOU CAN QUOTE ME"

OR THINKING OUTSIDE 'ONE'S INNER BOXER; IS TO 'FLOAT LIKE A BEE, AND 'STING LIKE A BUTTERFLY...

WHEREBY, IN THIS KIND OF A HUMAN RACE
MORALLY STRONG TOUGH GUYS FINISH FIRST.

- AS THIS 'MAVERICK PREACHER WILL TELL YOU; CAN 'YOU SAY THAT IT
TAKES ONE OF TREMENDOUS 'MORAL STRENGTH TO DO GOOD, OR RIGHT???

Train Like a Pro!

'A MENTAL HEALTH CARE, 'TEACHABLE MOMENT; MUSIC -ETC-

IT'S 'HOW ONE' KEEPS P.T.S.D ON A 'NEVER ADVANCING BACK BURNER.

DOCTOR'S BOOK OF NEW World **REMEDIES** IN BRIEF: 'A HOW TO 'COMBAT P.T.S.D GUIDE'
ALL CONTRIBUTING TO A **contagious -philosophy.**

'CASE IN STUDY, THE 11/18 CALIF; NIGHT CLUB KILLER,WAR VETERAN LONG. P.T.S.D.?
'RX' FIRST AND FOREMOST, GET YOURSELF A LOVING PET TO BE ONE'S BIG TIME MIND
CONSUMING RESPONSIBILITY FOR!!! 'OR' AS WAS STATED - THIS TRAGEDY COULD HAVE
ALL BEEN SET OFF BY WAY OF HIS FORMER GIRL FRIEND, LEAVING HIM FOR A DILDOE;
THUS TURNING HIM INTO A KILLING MACHINE; WHEREBY HEART BROKEN, AND IN NEED OF
SEXUAL THERAPY; HE SHOULD HAVE 'SPENT A LONG WEEKEND AT A WHORE HOUSE; AND BY
MONDAY MORNING HE WOULD HAVE NEVER REMEMBERED THE NAME OF THE GAL WHO SENT HIM.

"PHILLY CHEESE STEAK SANDWICH ANYONE? 'FOR ALL THOSE OUT THERE PROTESTING OPPOSITION TO THA DEATH PENALTY AT THA G.O.P, CONVENTION! 'MAD ENOUGH TO ■■■ ■■■ I SURE WISH I, WAS OUT THERE VIBRANTLY PREACHING AND PROTESTING RIGHT ALONG SIDE THEM; STATING! 'FOR THA LOVE OF GOD' THIS WILL BE THA ONLY WAY TO TRULY RID SOCIETY OF THA DEATH PENALTY., BECAUSE "FOR THA TRUE PERSONAL LOVE OF GOD,— THEIR CRIMES THAT GOT THEM THA DEATH PENALTY, WOULD HAVE NEVER HAPPENED."

(THIS IS NOT A / "HE DIED FOR OUR SINS, SO LET'S GO FOR THA GUSTO KIND OF RELIGION!")

spiritual connection

"♪ EVERYTHINGS MADE TO BE BROKEN, I JUST WANT YOU, TO KNOW WHO I AM ♫"

SIGNED: EMANCIPATOR EXTRAORDINAR

IMPORTANT NOTICE

"OPEN SEASON ON COMMON FOLK CITIZENS"

" The Shots Still Echo "

Gunman fired point-blank at crying children in church

HISTORY ON DISPLAY

" Vegas shooter had lost money "

"FROM THE 'GET GO' EXACTLY WHAT 'I WROTE AND SAID ABOUT! - TOSS IN SHOWSTOPPER 'MEMO, PLUS GAMBLERS PRAYER ESSAY; WITH THIS HERE <u>PROMO</u> STORY FOR A KICKER."

'showcases the truth about what's happening behind the scenes 'WITH

A teachable moment' wake-up call Exhibit

CLOCK IS TICKING ON

'THIS THING IS NOT OVER'.

Honoring Divine Inspiration ?

The POSITIVE SPIRIT

long reach:

HOLY 'Ghost Stories' Word Power:

'SYNCHRONIZING OUR MORAL COMPASS'

'revolutionary crunch time' or Same **old** story different day !

Imagemakers "stop this cover-up."

"WHAT WE HAVE 'HERE IS A FAILURE TO COMMUNICATE"

" *The Gospel according to* **If you Build This** " (81)

Letters to the Editor RENO GAZETTE-JOURNAL

THANK YOU KINDLY FOR PUTTING THE FLAG IN NEWS PRINT, THIS IS A GREAT SERVICE TO THE COMMUNITY. I NOW DISPLAY THIS PROUDLY IN MY PLACE OF EMPLOYMENT., AS THIS HERE ESSAY IS DEDICATED TO ALL THE PEOPLE THAT LOST THEIR LIVES ON (911) AND THEIR FAMILIES, ALONG WITH ALL THE INNOCENT PEOPLE THAT WILL LOSE THEIR LIVES ONCE WE, GOD BLESS AMERICA? RETALIATE. IN AS FAR AS PURSUING THE GUILTY IS CONCERN, DON'T LET THE CANDY ASPIRATIONS OF THE PACIFIST HOLD JURY TO THESE NEGATIVE SPIRITED, DEGENERATIVE LOW-LIFERS, WE NEED TO RID THE PLANET OF. I GET THE STRANGEST FEELING THAT THIS NOW, ON GOING WAR IS GOING TO LOOK ALOT LIKE A CAPITAL ONE CREDIT CARD COMMERICAL STATING. "WHATS IN YOUR WALLET." ON NEW AGE AIR TRANSPORT-ATION SAFETY! I FEEL WE SHOULD USE PLAIN CLOTHES, MILITARY PERSONNEL ON PLANES, TO MAINTAIN LOW FLIGHT COST AFFORDABILITY. THIS WHOLE WEEK HAS BEEN LIKE LIVING IN A REAL LIFE BAD MOVIE TO ME. THUS WAKING UP AND CLICKING OUR SOULS TOGETHER. THERE'S NO PLACE LIKE AMERICA, THERE'S NO PLACE LIKE AMERICA!

"My Fellow Americans" ` SOME DAY ALL ONE, GOD BLESS AMERICA. 'Hallelujah'.

(82)

WAR ON TERROR – ATTACK on America

UNITED BY TRAGEDY – Tha effects of tha terrorist attacks on

SEPTEMBER 11, 2001 'day of infamy.

'A Picture of Gloom'

Face *to* Face a reflection of feelings answer **to** "INSTIGATORS OF HELL." RELIGIOUS FAILING ZEALOTS. 'showcases tha RADICAL ISLAMIC JIHADIST. **tha Rise of Real People** Preaching a Gospel of ANTIPATHY ! this HERE DETERRENT proposal BEING A TRUE TO MORALISTIC LIFE, UPSTAGING REALITY CHECK IN PROTECTING THA HOME FRONT." "NOT IN OUR BACK-YARD", will defeat fanatics". "IN THAT THA ONLY WAY TO WIN **This War** IS TO BRING DOWN THEIR BELIEF SYSTEM." THIS HERE BEING A HOW TO PRESENTATION! →

Writer Author mourns death of innocent. Q TODAY'S QUICK READ . TRIVIA stirs past

FAITH FORUM

What does your faith say about spanking?

ANSWERS TO – IN THIS CASE, TO THE MAX!!! →

Searching For 'Real' Closure?

'ON A MISSION FROM GODZILLA; WAKE-UP CALL, ACTION-STOPPER •

"I BELIEVE YOU CAN MAKE PEOPLE NICE."

enough to support the brain.

THIS HERE BEING A HOW TO GUIDE! YOURS TRULY, 1999

"TERRORIST" MASS MURDERERS, SERIAL KILLERS, ETC; 'DETERRENT PROPOSAL'
EXAMPLE: ORLANDO, FRANCE, TEX CHURCH, CHRIST CHURCH, PARKLAND, LAS VEGAS, ELPASO, ETC.!

The Horrors of BUSINESS AS USUAL TERRORISM.

"Open Season on Common Folk Citizens"

'SOMEONE MUST STAND UP TO OUR CLUELESS APOLOGETICAL GOVERNMENT; THEY
CAN'T PROTECT US' (VS) THESE WARP MINDED DESPICABLES! THEREFORE, =

WE'RE NOT GONNA TAKE IT ANYMORE BEGINS HERE!

TODAY'S BRIEFING "DETERRENT PROPOSAL"

PROMO EXAMPLE AN 'ALL-FAITHS' **mecca** FACING WEST

MULTI-BILLION DOLLAR,
'TOURISM PILGRIMAGE'
'NO PLACE LIKE HELL' SATANIC BURIAL GROUND,
(((D.N.A. "ETC" - OR NOT.)))
'SPIT ON YOUR GRAVE' REALISTIC CLOSURE,
HORRIFIC CRIME,
—— C-O-N-S-E-Q-U-E N-C-E-S ——
"DETERRENT PROPOSAL"

"MOCKED FOR ETERNITY"

'JUST A REMINDER "THY WILL" BE DONE ON EARTH, AS IT IS IN 'HELL.

' YOUR INFAMOUS NAME WRITTEN IN STONE FOR SERVICES RENDERED TO SATAN.
(((WITH A RECURRING 'MAKE YOUR DAY' CELEBRATORY HELL ACCOMMODATIONS RITUAL.)))

'HELL **"IF YOU BUILD THIS THEY WILL COME"** HELL'
JUST NORTH OF RENO, NV. OFF 395.
- A DAILY VISITING FIELD-DAY,.

'WE WILL OFFICIALLY BURY YOU' PROJECT EXTRAVAGANZA.
TO MAKE'UM THINK, IS TO MAKE'UM BLINK!

" we Can prevent tragedy."

(84)

Words Are tha Best Weapon

"TRUTH", is more POWERFUL THAN ANY MAN MAID BOMB OR NUCLEAR DEVICE, BECAUSE WHEN THA OPPOSITION READS THIS BOOK., — BOY ARE THEY going TO EXPLODE !

BEHIND "tha LINES 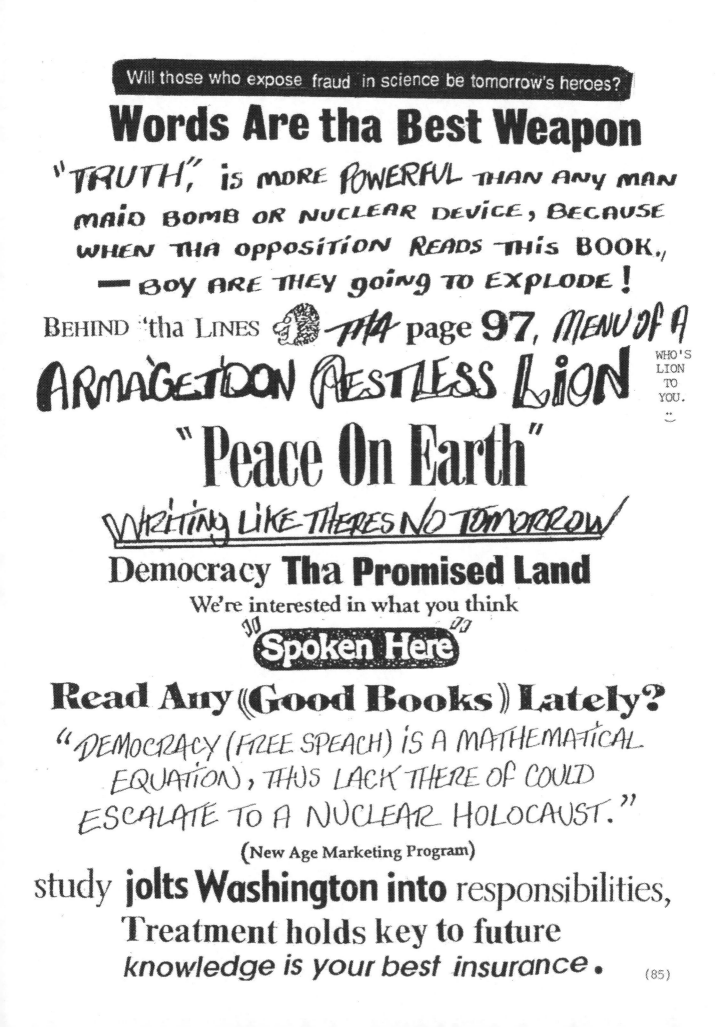 THA page 97, MENU OF A

ARMAGETDON RESTLESS LION

WHO'S LION TO YOU. :-)

"Peace On Earth"

WRITING LIKE THERES NO TOMORROW

Democracy Tha Promised Land

We're interested in what you think

"Spoken Here"

Read Any (Good Books) Lately?

"DEMOCRACY (FREE SPEACH) IS A MATHEMATICAL EQUATION, THUS LACK THERE OF COULD ESCALATE TO A NUCLEAR HOLOCAUST."

(New Age Marketing Program)

study **jolts Washington into** responsibilities, **Treatment holds key to future** *knowledge is your best insurance .*

(85)

Wing Commander WARFIGHTING ESSAY CONTEST

VISION Even Without A Flea Collar, *Written by* THA BARKING ANGEL *with* THA DOGMA, THAT HAS THA REAL BITE TO IT. **Page** *and moment is frozen in time.*

THE BOOK page 2B, OR NOT 2B. PAGE (86)

Millions spent to influence Congress

— Yeah, AND I'M JUST TRYING TO GET MY.2¢, WORTH IN!

CAMALOT, OR 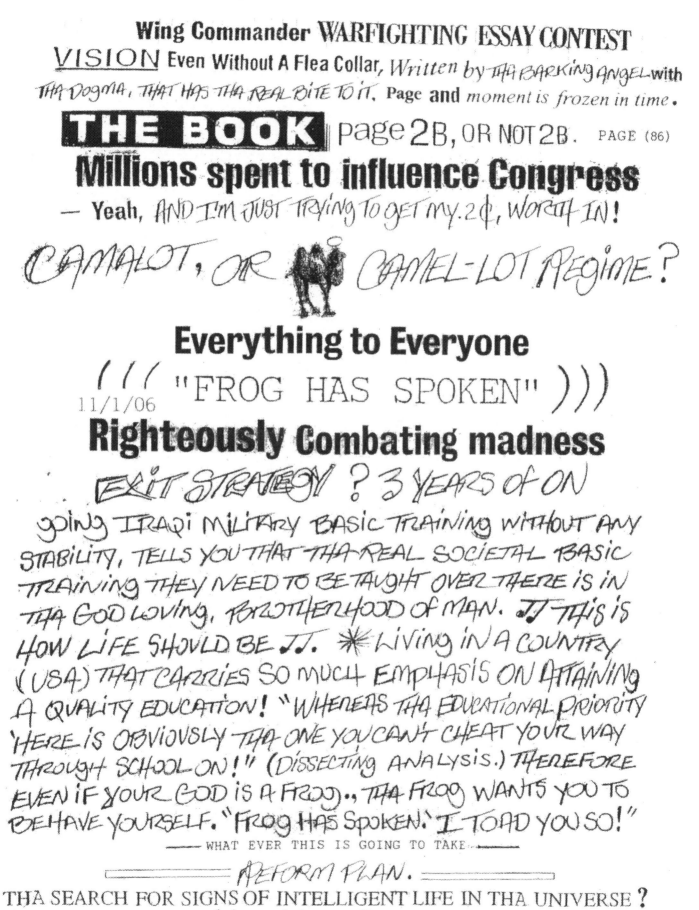 CAMEL-LOT REGIME?

Everything to Everyone

((("FROG HAS SPOKEN")))

11/1/06

Righteously Combating madness

EXIT STRATEGY? 3 YEARS OF ON GOING IRAQI MILITARY BASIC TRAINING WITHOUT ANY STABILITY, TELLS YOU THAT THA REAL SOCIETAL BASIC TRAINING THEY NEED TO BE TAUGHT OVER THERE IS IN THA GOD LOVING, FORBROTHERHOOD OF MAN. ♩♩ THIS IS HOW LIFE SHOULD BE ♩♩. ☀ LIVING IN A COUNTRY (USA) THAT CARRIES SO MUCH EMPHASIS ON ATTAINING A QUALITY EDUCATION! "WHEREAS THA EDUCATIONAL PRIORITY HERE IS OBVIOUSLY THA ONE YOU CAN'T CHEAT YOUR WAY THROUGH SCHOOL ON!" (DISSECTING ANALYSIS.) THEREFORE EVEN IF YOUR GOD IS A FROG., THA FROG WANTS YOU TO BEHAVE YOURSELF. "FROG HAS SPOKEN." I TOAD YOU SO!"

——— WHAT EVER THIS IS GOING TO TAKE ———

——— REFORM PLAN. ———

THA SEARCH FOR SIGNS OF INTELLIGENT LIFE IN THA UNIVERSE?

Yes, You Can...

in mlife **GETTING A WORD IN EDGEWISE.**

opinions **ON** Yucca Mountain decision.

'God Bless Afghanistan'

4700 MILLION DOLLARS IN TAX PAYER GIVE-AWAY SUPPORT? — AFTER PREP BOMBING THA MOUNTAINS OF AFGHANISTAN. "I THINK WE SHOULD STORE ALL OF OUR NUCLEAR WASTE IN THEIR BACK YARD. AFTER ALL — THEY'VE NEVER HAD ANY QUALMS ABOUT STORING ALL OF THEIR GROSS NATIONAL PRODUCT OPIUM, IN OURS."

Video against Yucca dump

shows a missile blasting a hole in a nuclear waste canister, potentially sending radiation into tha environment., footage could be used as part of a campaign to raise doubts about tha safety of shipping radioactive waste to Yucca Mountain.

POSITIVE (VERSUS) NEGATIVE **Not all monsters are make-believe.**

COLUMBUS-OSAMA BIN-LADEN, TOOK A CHANCE!

note worthy reviews **Something to Ponder** — DR. SUNDAY

— CAMPAIGN '92 EARTH SUMMIT **ON** State of Nevada RECEIVING NUCLEAR WASTE DUMPING! EITHER DUMP IT ON THA MOON. OR BETTER YET, — ROCKET THAT PUPPY INTO THA SUN. AN ARA FOREVER LOST? THEN SEND IT ALL TO CALIFORNIA, AND STORE THIS BEHIND THA HOLLYWOOD SIGN TO USE AS A BACK DROP IN A SCIENCE FICTION MOVIE. (87)

War & 'Peace' chapter :
long on substance, short on words.
Vintage Journalism

(((HISTORY REPEATS ITSELF)))'NAUGHTY ALLAH STRIKES AGAIN!
ISIS, ETC"

"EVIDENCE OF 'SATAN'S LITTLE HELPERS' IN NEED OF SCHOCK-THEARPY!"
'ONLY TRUTH CAN FREE YOU; FACTS SAVE LIVES'.
TO UTTER THE WORDS "G-OD IS GREAT" THEN TO
PRECEDE AND KILL INNOCENT PEOPLE TELLS ME,
THAT THESE EVIL-DOERS ARE STRONGLY
DEVOTED TO SERVING SATAN, OR IF YOU WILL THEIR INTO
S-A-T-A-N-TOLOGY.
♫ RAQQA AND ROLL IS 'NOT HERE TO STAY!
'RELIGION ALLAH CARTE - ISIS LEADER AL'BAGHDADI (VS) HOOSIER DADDY...
EXTRA - EXTRA - READ ALL ABOUT IT!!! JIHADIST LABOR DISPUT OF OVER 72 VIRGINS,
ENDS WHEN ORGANIZERS TOSS IN A FEW EXOTIC PORN STARS TO BREAK UP ALL THE MCNOTONY. ☺
- AS A SOCIETY WE'VE GONE FROM TERRORIST, TO BEING
LOOKED UPON AS ENEMY COMBATANTS, TO NOW BEING LOOKED
UPON AS ♫ MIDNIGHT AT THE OASIS-'NOT SO FRIENDLY!
(While You Were Out MESSAGE EXTENSION)

IN-BRIEF: **" ONLY GOODNESS 'POSITIVITY' COMES FROM GOD ".**
(((GULF SHOWDOWN PREDICTION)))
'FROM BAGHDAD TO BAGHLADY - BAATH PARTY TAKES A SHOWER!!!

DEAR
GADHAFI-DUCK,
'YOUR LIFE IS
LIKE THAT OF
YOU BEING A
CARTOON
CHARACTER,
YOU CAN'T BE
FOR REAL;
BECOME A HERO

SHOULD YOU FIND ANY?
"KILL WEAPONS OF MASS DESTRUCTION, NOT PEOPLE!"

(2012) **'Arab Spring**
'A NEW BAR OF SOAP THAT CLEANED
UP ON ALL THE SYRIAN REFUGEES"
(2008)
'HIGHLY IMPACTIVE
HISTORY
SHORTS
CONTINUED'
"INSTIGATORS" OF UN-HOLY-LAND;
BACKED BY POPULAR D-E-M-O-N-D;
'A RIGHTEOUS ROLLING STONE
GATHERS 'NO HAMAS!!!

AND LET THE FASHION POLICE ESCORT YOU OUT OF TOWN.
2008.VOTED NAY ON THE CLOSING OF GITMO---GITMO MILEAGE OUT OF IT.

:1991, CREATION OF A CONSCIOUS:

'DON'T YOU JUST WISH THAT THE SYRIAN LEADER ASSAD "ETC"
WOULD HAVE READ THESE`NEXT 2 PAGES, WAY BACK THEN. (88)

Warning "PLUTOCRATS" **Warning**

1st DRAFT OF ESSAY WAS WRITTEN IN 1982

YOU ARE WORTHY OF YOUR HOUSES,
YOU ARE WORTHY OF YOUR CARS,
IF THA (CON) IN CON-STITUTION CONTINUES
PLANET EARTH WILL SOME DAY BE ANOTHER MARS...
FOR CHRIST LURE CORPORATION SAKE,
WITH ANTICIPATION OF "HE WHO IS WITHOUT
SIN," CAST THA FIRST PAGE 90, NUCLEAR WAR
HEADS. NUCLEAR FREEZE IS SOMETHING THAT
THAWS OUT IN THA HEET OF ANOTHER
ARGUMENT. NUCLEAR ARMS RACE IS THA
TYPE OF (DIE)ALOGUE THAT WILL PROVIDE A
TRACK RECORD TO FINISHING DEAD LAST,
BECAUSE ALL YOUR DOING IS HORSING
AROUND BLIND JOCKEY. PAN HIDROSISLY, ARMS
CONTROL IS THA PIT'S. WHEREAS IGNORANCE
IS BLISTER, IN NUCLEAR WINTER WONDERLAND
FOR ALL US POTENTIAL UNKNOWN SOLDIERS
WITHOUT CEREMONY! SIGNED: CHARLY TUNA,
BECAUSE I'M ONLY TRYING TO SCHOOL YA., SO
WE ALL DON'T GET SON KISSED UNDER THA
MISSLE TOW

When Words Are tha Best Weapon: "Truth"

- IS MORE POWERFUL THAN ANY MAN MADE BOMB, OR NUCLEAR
DEVICE; BECAUSE WHEN THA OPPOSITION READS THIS BOOK,
BOY ARE THEY GOING TO EXPLODE!

Your guide to A kinder, gentler judgment day

(ANSWERS TO POSITIVE WORLD-INFORMATION to general public.)

BORN AND RAISED, I SALUTE MY COUNTRY USA., IN REGARDS TO DECEMBER 26TH, 2004. FOR WHEN A VAST MUSLIM REGION GOT HIT BY A DEVASTING TSUNAMI., TO THA RESCUE WE RESPONDED WITH BIG TIME ECONOMICAL SUPPORT, ETC! HUMBLING IN REALITY, BY WAY OF REVICTUALING THY BRETHREN, I LOVE THA SMELL OF HONOR THY NEIGHBOR IN THA MORNING! THEREFORE DID WE JUST BANK ON FOREIGN NEWS MEDIA TO FORETELL OF OUR KINDNESS AND GENEROSITY? IN OTHER WORDS DO THESE INSURGENTS EVEN HAVE A CLUE WE CAME FORTH WITH THIS KIND OF A NOBEL EFFORT? FURTHERMORE IF THA USA, DIDN'T INTERVENE IN BOSNIA, THERE WOULD BE NO MUSLIM COMMUNITY THERE. ALONG WITH UPHOLDING THA HISTORIC SOVEREIGNTY OF KUWAIT. (UP-DATED) 'I COULD HAVE STATED SOMETHING ABOUT US HELPING OUT WITH THA EARTH QUAKE VICTIMS IN PAKISTAN. From hear to eternity (ANSWERS TO WELCOME TO THA kinder, gentler BLESSINGS OF A 'DEMOCRATIZED CIVILAZATION!'"

You are now officially out of excuse.

WHAT DOES YOUR FUTURE LOOK LIKE?

"Great lessons in protests"

IN A Humane Society

you Do the right thing,

`Resistance must be heard´

deep thoughts on political issues

A mighty pen with a heart and soul

BY WAY OF ME PROVING TO YOU, THAT I'M THE MOST PROFICENT ACTOR THAT'S EVER
SET FOOT ON THE PLANET; PLAN ON IT. - LIVING IN A WORLD WHERE 'FOR SOME' IT'S
MORE SINFUL TO EAT BACON; THAN IT IS TO KILL AN INFIDEL. 'INTRODUCING THE ROCKET
SCIENCE SCHOOL THAT PRES. TRUMP NEVER GRADUATED FROM! 'THE MAKING OF AMERICA GREAT
AGAIN PART. (VS) 'THIS VOICE OF THE VOICELESS! 'GLOBABLE SPEAKING' IN AS FAR AS
'SANCTIONS' GO; I BELIEVE THAT THE LITTLE PEOPLE SHOULD 'NEVER' BE DENIED ANY
FOOD, MEDICAL, OR BASIC CLOTHING ACCOMODATIONS VIA ONE'S SANCTIONS. 'THE OPPO-
SITIONS LEADERSHIP NEVER WANT FOR ANYTHING! - IT'S JUST 'THEIR COMMON FOLK PEOPLE
THAT 'THEY DON'T REALLY CARE ABOUT IN THE FIRST PLACE THAT GET TO SUFFER. 'THUS
AN EASY EXCUSE FOR THEM NOT TO COMPLY WITH ANY DEMANDS. - AND WHAT'S SO GREAT ABOUT
ALL OUR MERCHANDISE BEING HELD BACK, THAT A PROPRIETOR HAS TO LAY-OFF WORKERS OF
$NEED IN OUR COUNTRY? - "ONLY IF IT'S 'SENSITIVE MATERIAL' SHOULD THERE EVER BE ANY
KIND OF A CLAUSE WITH CLAWS". "OVERALL TARIFF TRADE WARS" π WAR; WHAT IS IT GOOD
FOR? - ABSOLUTELY NOTHING! "PLANT TRADE NOT AID" - WHEREBY INFLATION' IS QUALITY
OF LIFES WORST NIGHTMARE. - WITH ALL THE WORK THAT THE MINIMUM WAGE PEOPLE MADE AN
EFFORT TO GAIN ON; BY WAY OF TARIFF INFLATION; YOU JUST DIG THEM BACK DEEPER INTO
POVERTY... (((NEXT))) 'FENCING WITH THE BEST OF THEM?!

POLITICAL POINTS OF VIEW.' **EFFECTIVE DIVERSIFICATION** matters.

YOURS TRULY SIGNED, **Customer SERVICE Representative** for

The voters nobody seems to know.

REVIEW & OUTLOOK **Ready to a-maze you.**

$\longrightarrow$

(92)

"Peace On Earth"

WRITTEN BY YOURS TRULY, IN 1991: ANSWERS TO TESTIMONIAL DOCUMENT SIGNING:

Tha Look-Ahead Factor *That Won't Go Away*

Reality Check *screening device for* presidential *candidates.*

(((GLOBALLY SPEAKING))) **When Hell Turned to Heaven!**

Tha Roads Not Taken—'so Crooks, Creeps and Cons Will Never Come to Power.'

If you are serious this could be tha

MOST IMPORTANT ad you will ever read.

'Peace' On Earth, Meet a Sales Counselor

Whose First Priority Is You. **Taking in Knowledge NOW & FOREVER —War** PAGE (93)

Tha greatest of sin (**versus**) *YOURS TRULY*, **Gospel Today** Peace Policy, **tha** meaning of life. **I** KNOW-WHEREOF-I-SPEAK; WE BY CHOICE ARE EITHER ON THIS HERE PLANET EARTH TO WILL FULLY SERVE ALMIGHTY God DILIGENTLY ., NOT THA CONTRARY. THUS UNIFYING THA REALITY OF Peace On Earth! policy remains firm. *This Certificate'* NO MORE WARS!

People from diverse cultures cooperate for understanding.

I HAVE READ, UNDERSTOOD, AND AGREE TO ABIDE BY GOD. sign oath!

name _ _ _ _ _ _ _ _ _ _ _ _ _ _ _ Date _ _ _ _ _

Big Read book
answers to
"Peace On Earth Sale"

Tha Birds And Tha Bees

'THE gospel According to Word Perfect
'All You Need Is a Match' PAGE (94)

"THA REALITY OF TRUE LOVE IS BUILT ON
A POSITIVE ((HONEST)) FOUNDATION."
IN ANY AMELIORATIVE SITUATION,
REFLECTIVELY FOR WHAT IS TRUTH — UNLESS
TWO PARTYS CAN AGREE UPON, YET APPLY TOO.

... And They Lived Happily Ever After

LOVE EDUCATION IS TRUE LOVES GAIN
AND WINNERS OF A Positive FOUNDATION GAME.
JORGE PILLER ASSAULT RELATIONSHIP IN A
BEAST ROW GARDEN OF YE DONE.

blame begins.

Lead us not into Shalt Nots,
UNCIVILIZED ABNORMALITYS ARE
THA CAUSE OF SOCIAL INFORMALITYS.

READINGS FOR REASONING

BREAKTHROUGH TRAINING !

SPECTRALLY, The one and only GOD THE
Positive SPIRIT; is MAN'S GREATEST TEACHER.

Professor's challenge is teaching
TOMORROW IN *Education TODAY*
writes from personal experience
1984 **IM PRUV ALL** Seminar
(QUESTIONS OF THA HEART) YOU Know

IT'S TIME TO START THINKING THAT THERE'S OTHER FISH IN THA SEA, WHEN INSTEAD OF FEELING THA PAIN OF ⟹ — CUPID'S ARROWS → YOUR ACTUALLY BEING HARPOONED. Better HOMES & GARDENS, Bingo **!** Lead us not into — UNCIVILIZED ABNORMALITYS, ARE THA CAUSE OF SOCIAL INFORMALITYS. Shalts and Shalt Nots, INITIALLY FOR 2 SO CALLED MATURE PEOPLE TO BE STRONGLY ATTRACTED TO ONE ANOTHER, THEN BY WAY OF THA CHANGE OF FACE BEHAVIORAL `game, END UP SETTLING FOR SOMEONE ELSE OUT OF THA SHEER SAKE OF FRUSTRATION, IS ABOUT AS SOCIAL FAILURE REWARDING AS —

Score THIS a Debate Knockout

→ STARTS WITH A HONORABLE MATCH, NOT A HONORABLE MENTION, BUT TO MENTION A CALCULATED OVERALL COMPATIBILITY PURSUIT GAME OF CONSIDERATION, TOWARD A BALANCED FLOW OF HONEST CIRCUMSTANTIAL TRUTH., DANCING TO THA BEAT OF THE RIGHT DRUMMER IS THA RIGHT BASIS OF A POSITIVE RELATIONSHIP, OR LOVE BOAT WITHOUT SINKING.

'MY FAVORITE Position
WITH A WOMAN IS WHEN I ⟹ (95)

STOP WONDERING. In This Fine Romance

What Makes Love Last? **In Memory of**

GOOD **OLD-FASHIONED** (Affection).

"WHAT'S MORE IMPORTANT THAN SEX IN A <u>MARITAL</u> RELATIONSHIP ? ANSWERS TO LONG HAUL AFFECTION SUPPORT, REASURRANCE !"

foresight Better Homes & Gardens.

'Two Can Play This Game, from tha book of love'.

INTIMATE LOVE IS NEVER TAKING ADVANTAGE OF THA ONE YOUR INTIMATE WITH, OR SEPERATION OF OWNERSHIP IS DOING FOR SOMEONE, NOT TO SOMEONE., FOR WHAT IS LESS, IS LESS THAN A HONORABLE Education.

As I see this Romance Is Here To Stay ◉

Heart to Heart
FAMILY VALUES
ACHIEVEMENT

in a *real world* environment

'**Contagious** Critique, Show of Shows'
Working Both Sides of tha Aisle
new book educator spells out vision ▪ (96)

INVOLVEMENT

PAST-THA LONELINESS IN A RELATIONSHIP ANYONE? THEREFORE THA PERFECT GAME MINUS PERFECT PLAYERS, WHEREAS TO LOOK FOR THA HONEST FACE YOU CAN FACE, AND BE CLEVER, IS THA HONEY MOON THAT WILL LAST FOREVER ...

Ladies and gentlemen, start your families. As I see this ONCE INTO A RELATIONSHIP, LONGEVITY IS **tha** GRANDEST WAY TO SERVE God •••

(vulnerabilities)

♪WELCOME TO THA HAVEN'T GOT TIME FOR THA PAIN ♯ MENTAL BLOCK CITY OF NO RETURN. CAUGHT UP IN A pulling away from **Trap** ! YOU ALWAYS WANT WHAT YOU DON'T HAVE, AND WHEN YOU GET IT, YOU DON'T WANT IT ANYMORE. <u>SUBCONSCIOUSLY</u> I'VE GOT YOU BABE♯ WHO'S NEXT ? SWEET ENDINGS AS FOR THIS REPORTERS OPINION ! I'D NEVER BE DUMB ENOUGH TO WALK AWAY FROM A GOOD SITUATION; FRANKLY SCARLET, "PERMIT"

"ONE DAY AT A TIME"

book of love 🎵 ' Setting *The* Agenda
Morals in a biblical tabloid
TAKING STOCK OF statement **Resolutions** put on paper,
pastor thinking outside the box !
TIMES ARE A CHANGIN'

TO ALL THE PEOPLE OUT THERE THAT ARE OPPOSED TO
THE 'LEGALIZATION OF PROSTITUTION'! GEAR UP FOR 'YOUR'
NOW NEW-AGE MORALITY SOCIETY! - NO MORE SUGAR DADDIES,
TROPHY WIVES,THUS NO MORE MARRYING SOMEONE BY WAY OF
THE 'WORLD'S OLDEST PROFESSION' "FOR THEIR MONEY".
'EVERYTHING IN LIFE IS TO A DEGREE' WHEREAS,
'BIG BROTHER SUBJECTS' YOU'LL NOW BE ASSIGN
TO A MARRIAGE BALANCED ECONOMIC ASSESSMENT CONCILIAR,
FOR YOUR MARRIAGE LEGITIMACY. ☺
'SO TO SPEAK, NEW-AGE MORALITY SOCIETY?!
- MANY A 'SAME 'STORY EXAMPLE OUT THERE
TO HAVING A 'NO THERAPEUTIC ACCESS
FOR A -CHO-SEUNG-HUI-KILL-32-;
WHO WAS A SEX DRIVEN CRAZED 'VIRGIN,
IN PERSUIT OF BECOMING A
'I'LL JUST PAY FOR IT' ROLL IN THE HAY
* REJECT ●
'THUS RESULTING IN HIM BECOMING A KILLING MACHINE.
FURTHERMORE, WITH THE 'HISTORY OF ALL THE SEXUALLY
ASSAULTED VULNERABLE WOMEN IN THE U.S. MILITARY;
JUST THE SAME, TOSS IN ALL THE COLLEGE CAMPUS
'LOWER EDUCATION'GO FOR IT' ACCESSIBILE COVER-UP FACILITIES.
WHEREBY, IN TAKING AWAY ALL THE DIM-WIT PREDATORS EXCUSES;
THERE'S NO EXCUSE FOR THAT KIND OF MISCREANT BEHAVIOR
ANYMORE...
'SUMMERY, SUMMARY' IN CONCLUSION:
"LEGALIZE PROSTITUTION"

Based on Notebooks 'Plan for Prosperity'
As Book lovers gear up for sale

EVERYONE'S TALKING ABOUT IT

FEATURING WE NEED TO OPEN
THIS WHOLE CAN OF WORMS TO THE FULLEST EXTENT
IF WE'RE GOING TO BE CULTURALLY RECTIFYING
ALL OF CIVILIZATION.
IN BRIEF EXAMPLE: BETTER CLERGY?
DEVIL FORBID! WHAT IF?
'TO BECOME A CATHOLIC PRIEST ETC,
TO GET IN; YOU NOW HAVE TO SWEAR OFF CHILDREN,
AS OPPOSED TO WOMEN! ☺

'TIME AND PLACE FOR EVERY WARDROBE'
"STILL NO EXCUSE FOR #METOO SEXUAL MISCONDUCT".
～ POINSETTIA AND THEN SOME...

⇒ CLUELESS TAUNTING BY WOMEN, IS WHEN THEY ARE
INAPPROPRIATELY DRESSED TO SEXY FOR THE OCCASION;
THAT CAN LEAD TO ～THIS AN EFFECT. IN HINDSIGHT A HOW TO:
MAKE GUY'S ACKNOWLEDGE YOU FOR YOUR 'NANCY PELOSI
WARDROBE; SHOULD YOU WANT TO BE LOOKED UPON AND
ACKNOWLEDGED FOR WHAT'S BETWEEN YOUR EARS, AS OPPOSED
TO WHAT'S BETWEEN YOUR ARM PITS.'ETC'
'EVERYBODY IS SELLING SOMETHING':

Front Lines **Sounding Retreat** '
ULTIMATE PLAYGROUND "Games PEOPLE PLAY?"
'morality?' **Woman Behaving Badly!**

Explosive Story Of Dramatic, Authentic Original Combat " Circle tha Wagons!"
Lasting Impressions, WAR PAINT AT DAWN:
CUSTER'S LAST STAND

'WOMEN ARE GOING TO HAVE TO BE MORE RESPECTFUL WHEN
BEING CHASED BY MEN, INTHAT SHOULD YOU HAVE No Interest
IN YOUR PURSUER! BECOME OBVIOUS TO THA FACT THAT
THIS PORCUPINE'S PROBABLY GOT MORE OF CUPID'S ARROWS
STICKING IN HIM, THEN GENERAL CUSTER. NEVER LET HIM
OVER STAY HIS VIST, OR STRING HIM OUT FOR A LONG PERIOD OF TIME.

"Tha World According to
a LEGALIZE Prostitution proposal"
READING REVOLUTION
"Storytelling on a grand scale"
"STEMMING FROM THA WAR BETWEEN THA SEXES."

Learning from tha past, a study in history

Thanks for tha memories

NO, DON'T GET ME WRONG. I'M NOT TRYING TO CHANGE ALL THOSE **Fool** CAN'T CATCH ME, SHALLOW LOW SELF-ESTEEM GAMES PLAYED BY THA EVERY DAY WOMEN OF SOCIETY! PLEASE DO. I'M ONLY TRYING TO COMPENSATE FOR THEM! **Nobody's Fool** PLEASE DO LEGALIZE

PROSTITUTION **All things being equal.** BEHAVIORALLY SPEAKING, OR VENGING ONE'S FRUSTRATIONS AND HAVING **NO** OUT-LET FOR, IT'S TIME TO FACE ALL THA UNLAWFUL EMOTIONAL AND PSYCHOLOGICAL SPIN-OFFS, SURROUNDING THIS HERE LONG IN THA TOOTH ISSUE.

GIRL OF THA MONTH CLUB, OR RICHTER SCALE

LYING ONE NIGHT STANDS;

Uncover tha real truths about abortion

CRUCIAL POINT HAS BEEN OVERLOOKED:

' bullseye, MANY AN ABORTION WOULD HAVE NEVER TAKEN PLACE."

STUDIES INDICATE PUT AN END TO SEXUAL HARASSMENT IN THA WORK PLACE!!!
- WHEREAS THIS PROPOSAL WOULD GIVE EVEN A 'DARK SIDE OF LIFE' RAPIST <u>AN OPTION</u>;
AS LIKE IN TURTLE HEAD LOOKING <u>HARVEY WEINSTEIN</u> 'ETC'
WHO SEEMS TO THINK THAT 'ALL RAPE IS CONSENSUAL SEX'
AND THAT RESISTANCE TO IT IS, NOTHING MORE THAN EXCITABLE FORE-PLAY... :(

Unforgettable Moments.

(100)

<u>Inside</u>**today** A 'Monster' Awakening

SEEING THA WORLD THROUGH DR. WEARING HEART ON SLEAVES EYE'S. GAMES **and War Stories from tha Field.**

(FEATURES BEAUTY AND THA BEAST!) IN PURSUIT, OR A VESTED TIME EXPERIENCE EXAMPLE: "IN MY MIND", SHE WAS THA FOXEST LOOKING GAL THIS SIDE OF TONOPAH!

ALL MEN ARE JERKS

JUST NOW TAKING CAT NAPS OR LION ON THA MEND, "AFTER TAKING ALL THA BATE" AND FOAMING AT THA MOUTH, AS SHE WALKED AWAY FROM ME, PUTTING ME ON HELL HOLD FOR ETERNITY. I WAS ALREADY HAVING A BAD HAIR DAY, OR PUTTING THA POTENTIAL MONSTER IN ME MILDLY, I ALMOST SNAPPED, AFTER BEING JERKED AROUND, SHE ALONG WITH A LOT OF OTTERS PAWING ON HER, WOULD HAVE FOUND OUT QUICK THAT I WAS THA REAL 'NO MORE MR. NICE guy OF HER DREAMS. **PLAN B.** **Truck Load of Mattress!**

THUS BEING A FAITHFUL SERVANT TO THE ALMIGHTY, OR MY BEST FRIEND. I <u>WIMPED OUT THA DOOR HOPING I'D RUN</u> INTO A RAGING FRENZY OF (((LEGALIZE PROSTITUTION))) BROKEN HEARTED TO THA MAX, <u>I'LL GET OVER YOU!</u> test of time, this **IS MY BRAIN ON HEART - CORE - REJECTION.**

BROKEN HEARTS! <u>THIS WAS THEIRS.</u> Suicide SPOUSAL CRIME, "ETC". DRUGS, TRAFFIC FATALITYS, <u>FOR</u> <u>THIS</u> <u>COVERS</u> <u>A DEVIL</u> <u>AWFUL</u> LOT-OF-CEMETERY-GROUND— **DID YOU KNOW A BROKEN** ♡ WITH A NOT SO HAPPY ENDING ? ?

(101)

NOTICE TO THE PUBLIC

EVEN UNDER THA BEST OF CIRCUMSTANCES

A good portion of society's adults arn't cut out for long term relationships be it one reason, or another ,, inthat if one lived to be 900 years old, and never found their match, one could atleast be a functionally productive piller of tha commune type citizen. PAGE

issue persist, **come to terms** WITH

THA OVER-ALL Dignity OF A |HISTORY of

politicians ! A **SHOCK & STRUT**

proposal WITH A HAPPIER ENDING.,,

–AS OPPOSED TO 'ALL THA EVERY DAY GAL'S THAT WERE JUST TAKEN FOR A RIDE...

Establishing Service ON HORIZON Just add sales tax, Nelly.

'Excuse me, Living within this a sell it with sex, sexually overtoned media environment. 'GET REAL AND ROCK STAR EVERYBODY, with **prostitute** 'Two-Minute Drill'.

NATION WIDE RURAL · RURBAN PROPOSAL Innovation: OUT A Sight ! INCORPORATE THIS AREA ADULTS ONLY. ALONG WITH ALL THA TOPLESS BARS, **X** RATED MOVIE HOUSES, ADULT SOFT PORN MAGAZINES, MOTELS, AND CALL THIS AREA SIN CITY.

(NBC, TV.) DATE LINE, FEED BACK:

JANUARY 25, 2000 IN REFERENCE TO DEFINING

RAPE! INEXCUSABLE, FELONIES RAPE, IS A

SEXUALLY OFFENSIVE CRIME AS OPPOSE

TO THA OLD STANDARDIZED CONTROL FREAK ISSUE.

IMPERATIVELY "RAPE IS SEXUAL RAGE".

A DECISIVE OR SPONTANEOUS REACTION,

STEMMING FROM ONE'S OWN ILLICIT,

OVER-POWERING, SELF-GRATIFICATION OF A

SEXUALLY FRUSTRATED INDIVIDUAL,

IN EVIDENCE OF A SPERM WHALE.

The Strength of Advice
WITH A VOICE COMMAND.

ANALYSIS SIGNED BY- PUSH -IN-DOCTOR
DR. GLADIMIR INSTEADOFDARE
RX TAKE 2 PROSTITUTES, AND CALL ME IN THA MORNING.

'A MAKE A DIFFERENCE
ENDER'S GAME'
You Can Believe In . (103)

'MONK AMONG YOU'

lifestyle OnAssignment

OR " RELIGIOUSLY MARRIED tO my VOCATION."

process clarify / obligation with God., meets

with clients. meets with unlimited.'A EVERY

DAY intimate lOVING RELATIONSHIP iS

a matter of Having adequate time!

(First draft of An event is born)

true PREPARATION Can find a place for Love

and Romance In This a BUSY LIFESTYLE!

Who's Tha Right One For You?

Help Wanted: needed A Unique COVER GIRL

Attraction with 'Adaptation' of turning into

A Multitasker LIVE=IN SECRETARY-MAID

and then some.,'Can you hear me now

Girl friend'. WHAT NO TAKERS? PAGE BUNNY RANCH.

RENO NEVADA, He's not worried-Go for

plan B, backup project Proposal!

DOCTOR'S BOOK OF NEW World REMEDIES

IT'S A NO-BRAINER ... PAGE (104)

Birds And Bees   (POEM) ENTITLED,
Love On Course

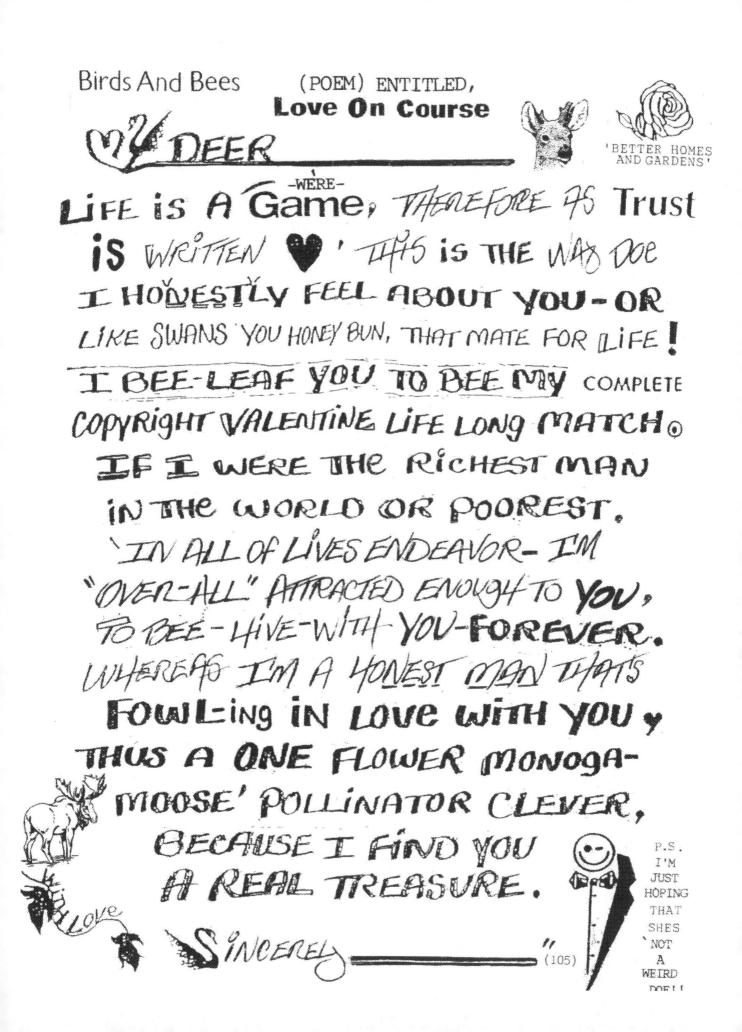

MY DEER _____

-WERE-

LIFE is A Game, THEREFORE AS Trust
iS WRITTEN ♥' THIS is THE WAY DOE
I HONESTLY FEEL ABOUT YOU-OR
LIKE SWANS YOU HONEY BUN, THAT MATE FOR LIFE!
I BEE-LEAF YOU TO BEE MY COMPLETE
COPYRIGHT VALENTINE LIFE LONG MATCH☉
IF I WERE THE RICHEST MAN
IN THE WORLD OR POOREST.
`IN ALL OF LIVES ENDEAVOR- IM
"OVER-ALL" ATTRACTED ENOUGH TO YOU,
TO BEE-HIVE-WITH YOU-FOREVER.
WHEREAS I'M A HONEST MAN THATS
FOWL-ing IN LOVE WITH YOU,
THUS A ONE FLOWER MONOGA-
MOOSE' POLLINATOR CLEVER,
BECAUSE I FIND YOU
A REAL TREASURE.

WITH LOVE

SINCERELY _____" (105)

P.S.
I'M
JUST
HOPING
THAT
SHES
`NOT
A
WEIRD
DOE!!

'BETTER HOMES
AND GARDENS'

THA CHANGING FACE OF It's All Good

NO DEFENDING THA CAVEMAN — "LIFE BEGINS AT 50!"

LONELINESS is cutting off your ear, and never getting discovered. :)

LONELINESS NEVER HAS TO WORRY ABOUT THA LIFE EXPECTANCY OF EFFORTLESS FORE PLAY, NOR A SPOUSE THATS OUT HAVING AN AFFAIR. THUS LONELINESS NEVER PLAYS ANYBODYS FOOL, OR MEAL TICKET... LONELINESS AT HOME, COMES AND GOES WITHOUT ANSWERING TO ANY PERSON... PERSE LONELINESS NEVER GETS V.D, HERPES, AIDS, OR NEEDS AN ABORTION CLINIC...

LONELINESS IS NEVER BEING A PARENT PAGE HAVING TO EXPLAIN WHY YOU BROUGHT THEM INTO THIS WORLD OF UNFAIRNESS... SIGNED ANONYMOUS, LONELINESS ALWAYS SIGNS THAT WAY...

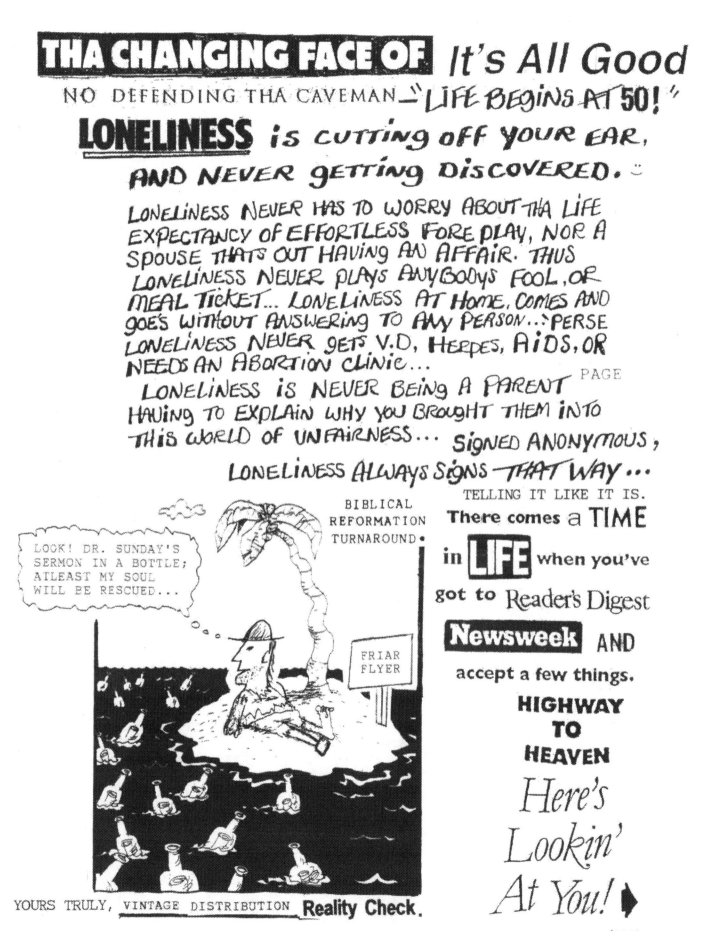

BIBLICAL
REFORMATION
TURNAROUND

TELLING IT LIKE IT IS.
There comes a **TIME** in **LIFE** when you've got to Reader's Digest **Newsweek** AND accept a few things.

HIGHWAY TO HEAVEN

Here's Lookin' At You! ◆

LOOK! DR. SUNDAY'S SERMON IN A BOTTLE; ATLEAST MY SOUL WILL BE RESCUED...

FRIAR FLYER

YOURS TRULY, VINTAGE DISTRIBUTION **Reality Check.**

CHARTING A NEW COURSE

playing Positive **Games** 'Shalts and Shalt Nots'

Morals in a biblical tabloid

Adding up tha costs — **Mystique no more**

EXCRUCIATING, WHEN You Can't Tell tha Players

IN A WORLD THAT HASN'T THA FOGGIEST

IN ITS TEACHINGS OF HOW TO ATONE ONE'S

LIFE LONG MATCH THRU CIVILIZED COURTING.

Ah Yes, I Remember Them Well.

book of love 𝄞 ' Setting *Tha* Agenda

Time Well Spent Serving Your Needs

Don't you wish you had seen this ad in 19 - ?

— AND DEAR GOD, According To BOOK'S
OVERALL CURRICULUM, 'NO NEED TO FORGIVE ANY-
ONE NOW; FOR THEY KNOW NOW WHAT THEY DO!'

(((OR PARALLELS BEST ONE-UPMANSHIP.)))

**A tale of two testaments comes
alive**. Project Community *INDIVIDUAL*

RESPONSIBILITY, **Welcome to tha Neighborhood!**

Thumbs up ready to preach to *Tha* masses

GIVING CREDIT *Exceeding Expectations*

How do you like me now? PAGE (107)

True Redemption.

Tuesday, March 31, 1992

"YES! WERE A RARE BREED US SPORTS FANS A GOOD PORTION OF US REJECTED PROFESSIONAL ATHLETES AND COACHES FOR ONE REASON OR ANOTHER, BEING PERFECT MOMENTUM CHANGING TIME OUT WIZARDS, ARM CHAIR QUARTERBACKS, AND PITCHING CHANGE EXPERTS.

I'LL ALWAYS RECALL MY MOST INSPIRATIONAL MOMENT IN SPORT. THA 1976 NCAA FOOTBALL NATIONAL CHAMPIONSHIP GAME. SPORTSCASTER KIETH JACKSON. "CATHOLICS VERSUS PROTESTANTS, NORTH VERSUS SOUTH, NOTRE DAME VERSUS BAMA. THESE ARE THA WARS THAT WERE MENT FOR MAN-KIND." HAVING NO FAITH IN MYSELF AND ONLY IN THE GOD I SERVE, THAT STATEMENT WAS ONE OF MY GREATEST COMMUNIONS IN FORMULATING MY IDEOLOGY TO THA REALITY OF UNDERSTANDING MANKIND.

"WORLD SERIES, OR WORLD SERIOUS. BRIEFLY, HOW MANY CUBAN AND SOUTH AMERICAN BASE BALL PLAYERS AWAIT THESE SAME OPPORTUNITYS. $HOW MANY ASPIRING SANDY KOUFAX'S DO WE HAVE IN ISRAEL, OR ROCK THROWING KID'S IN THA GAZA STRIP THAT COULD, PIECE OF CAKE THROW RICKEY HENDERSON OUT AT SECOND. $HOW MANY PERSIAN OR RUSSIAN WEIGHT LIFTING MEAT HEADS, DO WE HAVE THAT COULD PUT A LAWRENCE TAYLOR ON HIS BACK IN PROTECTING A QUARTERBACK etc.

PEACE ON EARTH?

THA FAMILY THAT PLAYS TOGETHER, STAYS TOGETHER.

WRITTEN BY: AT ONE TIME AN ASPIRING FOOTBALL COACH THAT CAME TO REALIZE IN THA REAL GLOBAL FIELD OF PLAY, THAT THA WHOLE STADIUM COULD USE SOME GOOD COACHING ...

Read Any ((Good Books)) Lately?

EVERYONE HAS A POTENTIAL
<u>GOOD</u> BOOK IN THEM; IF THEY
COULD ONLY FIND A <u>GOOD</u> INTERPRETER...

Vintage Journalism

READINGS FOR REASONING

survivability plus growth

an <u>IN Brief</u> PERSPECTIVE on EARTHQUAKES

Amid tha ruins, blame begins

THA GLOBAL WORLD IS A FUNCTIONAL BODY ACTING MUCH LIKE YOUR VERY OWN., TO SUCK OUT IT'S LIFE BLOOD (OIL) IN A SENSITIVE FAULT AREA, IS ASKING FOR BIG TROUBLE! GOING GREEN ANYONE?` WHILE I'M ON THA SUBJECT OF (OIL) WITH ALL OF THESE WORLD WIDE POLLUTING OIL SPILLS, THA ENVIRONMENTALLY SAFE WAY TO GO WOULD BE IN USING DOUBLE BELLY OIL TANKERS, THUS A WORTHY COST EFFECTIVE CONSUMER MARKET TAKE-OVER WAITING TO HAPPEN.., SO WHERE DID I GET ALL MY INFORMATION?` I DID STAY AT A HOLIDAY INN EXPRESS LAST NIGHT., **or** FROM THE

WIDE-EYED AND FOCUSED I'LL NEVER FORGET THAT SUNDAY MORNING WHILE WATCHING THA TV NEWS, AND HAVING BREAKFAST., THA METEOROLOGIST FORECASTING 175 MILE AN HOUR WINDS, THAT ARE HEADED STRAIGHT TOWARDS NEW ORLEANS, AND DUE TO LAND IN APPROXIMATELY 24 HOURS, FROM NOW! `KNOWING THAT AND THAT, THA LEVEE'S WERE ABOUT AS SAFE AS, A ALL-TERRAIN MARATHON RUNNER ENTERING A RACE WEARING CARD-BOARD FLIP-FLOPS., — I KNOW MYSELF I, WOULD HAVE ATLEAST BATTEN DOWN IN BATON ROUGE!

forcasting **TAKEOFF POINT :** <u>UPON 1ST ALERT, ANITA</u> — <u>HUMUNGOUS CONVOY</u> OF BUSES READY TO GO!

AFTERMATH HELICOPTER OBSERVATION : IN REGARDS TO ALL OF THA PEOPLE THAT WERE STRANDED AT THA CONVENTION CENTER ETC. —`GROUND CONTROL TO MAJOR TOM! WE ANITA — MASSIVE AERIAL DROP OF FOOD, (MRI'S) WATER, PORTA-POTTIES, ETC.

Spreading tha Blame ?

`` `BLAME IT ON THA BOSSA-NOVA! POSITIVE RAIN, NEGATIVE RAIN, ATMOSPHERIC POSITIVE, ATMOSPHERIC NEGATIVE. CREATIVE CURRENTS! `BLAME IT ON THA RIO DE JANEIRO, <u>FALSE GOD, SON</u>-WORLD, WORSHIP EXHIBIT! ''

'THIS THING IS NOT OVER'
When words need to be said
Poor People's Campaign
To the letter

NEW-AGE PHILOSOPHY PROPHECY,'SHOULD THIS BE YOU'
FEATURING THE BABY FACTORY, TOTAL IRRESPONSIBILTY
S-I-N-DROME PLAYERS!
DOES THIS NEEDLE POINT TO YOU?
'THUS BEING A MISERY LOVES COMPANY CONTRIBUTOR.
WHEREAS, BRINGING SOMEONE AS LIKE IN YOURSELF,
INTO THIS WORLD THAT WILL ALWAYS HAVE TO STRUGGLE
FOR FOOD, CLOTHING, SHELTER, ETC, VIA
THE WHOLE QUALITY OF LIFE PACKAGE.

Call Time Out!

'GLOBALLY
SPEAKING'

'BIRTH CONTROL IS A
REALISTIC DIFFERENCE MAKER'
- OR -

WELCOME TO 'HELL'
MAKE SURE THEY ISSUE YOU
A PITCH'FORK...

THEREFORE, GO FORTH AND MULTIPY THIS PHILOSOPHY;
'WHY BE STUCK IN THIS 'HELLISH

- 'YOU GET TO SUFFER, SUFFER , TILL YOU DIE SOCIETY.,
WAREHOUSE POOL OF = OVERPOPULATION, GREENHOUSE GASSES,
RESOURCE EXHAUSTING 'THE BEAT GOES ON' OVERLOAD;
WHERE THE EMPLOYER, HAS THE VAST LUXURY OF PICK AND
CHOOSE PERSONEL; WHEN 'YOU CAN HAVE THE LESS SUPPLY
THE MORE DEMAND LUXURY OF EVENTUALLY ENTERING INTO
THE 'HURRAY FOR ME,'I GOT MINE SOCIETY' THAT FORMULATES
'QUALITY OF LIFE $EQUALITY...

(((RIDDING THE WORLD OF EVENTUALLY HAVING TO EAT OCEANS FILLED WITH PLASTIC FISH.)))

TIMES ARE A CHANGIN'

'FOR THOSE OF YOU THAT LOVE KIDS SO MUCH; 'THERE'S A SPECIAL
PLACE IN HEAVEN' THAT GOD, PUT YOU ON THIS EARTH TO PERFORM;
IT'S CALLED SCHOOL TEACHER...

(112)

"**When words need to be said**"
The **Future of** earth balance
democracy is at stake.
POLLUTION:
World's No. 1 killer
a threat to mankind?
questioning authority

'SO YESTERDAY' FOR THEIR FAILURE TO RECOGNIZE THE 'EQUAL IMPACT OF –

What EVERYONE ON EARTH Needs to KNOW.

Birth control is A Realistic Survival Plan.

"OVERPOPULATION IS A MAJOR IN-GREEDY-ENT TO GLOBAL WARMING CLIMATE CHANGE"

SCIENCE, **lack of ability to 'go deep' leading to**

hellish conditions
Libra (Sept. 23-Oct. 23).
The advances in thought come
when you mix categories.

: Earth in danger earth **at stake.**

'WITH EXAMPLE OF WARM WATER HURRICANES, DEATH ☹ AND DISTRUCTION $$$

time to calculate the costs?

Point-of-View *PRO-LIFE GOES INTO EFFECT THE DAY*
PRO-INTELLIGENCE, (BIRTH CONTROL) COMES OF AGE.
' **CHOOSE** *PRO-INTELLIGENCE.'*
oF Paradise & Poverty

IRRESPONSIBILITY CULMINATES TO THIS HERE BEING A GLOBAL RESOURCE EXHAUSTING
'BABY FACTORY' POVERTY STRICKEN OVER-LOAD OF =BIBLICAL PROPORTIONS=!
-FETUS-FEED-US-FEET-US- (SHOES, etc. -FEAT-US-(JOBS, JOBS, JOBS,).

2012, THERE'S NO SUCH THING AS OVER-
POPULATION AND PIECE ON EARTH; THE MORE THE SCARIER. (EXAMPLE)
'ARAB SPRING' IN SYRIA, 'ETC! IN REFERENCE TO THE KILLING OF ALL
THOSE PEOPLE'-IN NOT BEING ABLE TO PROVIDE FOR THEIR WANTS AND
NEEDS, THEY ALL BECAME 'EQIVALENT' TO A HOUSE CLEANING LATE TERM
ABORTION; ALONG WITH ALL THE MULTITUDES OF TENT CITY REFUGEES,
THAT ARE ALL PRODUCTS OF 'OVERPOPULATION' THUS
AN UN-ACHIEVABLE QUALITY OF LIFE'S WORST NIGHTMARE!   (113)

"LEADERSHIP" SHOWCASE

♫♪ MA-MA, DON'T LET YOUR BABIES GROW-UP TO BE COW'ARDS. ♪♫

Americans still want people of faith as leaders.

"THEREFORE SINGING IN ACA-PULCO, 'HERE I COME TO SAVE THA DAY.'"

IN REPRESENTING AMERICA, ITS IMPORTANT TO HAVE VARYING POLITICAL POINTS OF VIEW. **WHO'S NEWS:** is Door opening for this religious **ACTION HERO** overachiever?

story REFLECTION Just Listen To What He's Saying —

Warns against 'political cowardice' of, **or** inaction. REACH OUT AND SHOCK SOMEONE. **i condemn**

THA DEMOCRACY OPPRESSING POLITICAL AND MEDIA COWARDS IN THIS COUNTRY RESTING ON THEIR LAURELS AND HARDY, ALONG WITH THEIR INABILITY TO CREATE SOCIOECONOMIC DIGNITY AMONG THA IMPOVERISHED.

BOOK PROPOSED

TAKEOFF POINT "responsibility". IT appears THAT WITHOUT A ACTIVATED 3RD PARTY, WHISTLE-BLOWING WATCH DOG ENTITY., THA COMMON FOLK TAX PAYER DOLLAR WILL ALWAYS BE SUBJECT TO LOBBIED INSIDER, MAFIA-STYLE - 'WE KNOW WHATS GOOD FOR YOU' EXTORTION!

WHEREAS THIS IS MY IDEA OF A BIG-TIME ELIOT NESS, OPERATION...

"NO! I'M NOT TRYING TO PUT THA A.A. OR ANY AFFILIATED COMPANY OUT OF BUSINESS. I'M ONLY TRYING TO GET THEM TO PREACH WHAT I PREACH." ALCOHOLISM IS 'NOT A DISEASE.' IT'S A CONDITIONING FACTOR OF ABUSIVE DRINKING BY A INDIVIDUAL CAUGHT UP WITHIN A PATTERN OF IRRESPONSIBLE DRINKING HABITS, OR REPEAT PERFORMANCES; IN THAT THIS INDIVIDUAL IS GENERALLY SELF CENTERED TO A POINT, WITHOUT REALIZING YOU CAN'T SERVE GOD, THROUGH YOUR FELLOW MAN, AND ABUSE ALCOHOL. (((FREQUENT FLYER END GAME.)))

An exclusive book excerpt.

HAPPY NEW YEAR, 365:

Puts _You_ in tha Driver's Seat!

A LITTLE DAB WILL DO YA, IS A HIGHER FORM OF INTELLIGENCE. PROJECTING MIND OVER MATTER, AS OPPOSE TO INTOXICATING MATTER OVER MIND! PRETENTIOUSLY, THIS MAN'S RELIGION IS INTO (CLONING) WORDS IN THEIR MOUTHS.
RE-MONSTRA-TIVELY FALLING PREY TO LETTING YOUR 'SHOULDER DEVIL' TAKE THA WHEEL, CAN RESULT INTO SOME HORRIFYING CIRCUMSTANCES.
"DEVIL IN THA DETAILS— NOWHERE TO HIDE".
EXCESSIVE USE OF ALCOHOL WHILE DRIVING IS LIKE A (WOE IS ME) 'OR PARTY ANIMAL' D.U.I. DEATH DEFYING SELF-CENTERED-SIN-DROME ANYONE??? CARD HOLDERS CLUB 'SHOWCASE EXPOSURE' ANSWERS TO WHAT'S REALLY HAPPENING BEHIND THESE TRAGIC SCENES. (115)

What is your moral argument on assisted suicide?

Commentary ON Terminal Care:
Too Painful, Too Prolonged
HAVE STORIES TO TELL.

OPINION ON DR. JACK KEVORKIAN'S assisted right-to-die

'Politically corrected' "TERMINAL MERCY. MADE FOR

I STAND IN FAVOR OF, AS LONG AS WE GET A 2ND QUALIFIED DOCTORS OPINION! THIS WAY WE CAN ALWAYS REFER BACK TO (WITCH) DOCTOR... ☺

Health REPORT Best idea whose time has come

On individual suffering that comes with a degenerative disease., Or penniless vegetating old; old people who wish to end their lives. "It's pretty ghoulish when people shoot themselves with guns ETC." knowledgeable in all aspects of "Terminal mercy"

FREEDOM OF CHOICE From human misery!

"provide a humane alternative, Create a pill." DR. SUNDAY.

Vintage Journalism

TIME CAPSULE— ON NASA space shuttles

ECONOMIC PRIORITIES! OTHER THAN SATELLITE COMMUNICATIONS ETC, DON'T EXPECT TO GET A WHOLE LOT OF SUPPORT $ FROM YOURS TRULY., UNLESS NASA GOES FUNKY AND NAMES THA NEXT SPACE SHUTTLE SOMETHING LIKE "RICH MANS TOY." PRIVATE ENTERPRISE THEY'RE CALLING YOUR NAME. Written by A FORMER BEACH FRONT PROPERTY SALESMAN FOR MARS. MORALLY SPEAKING **Shattering beliefs** NOBODY TAKES OFF THEIR SPACE SUIT AND GOES SKINNY DIPPING, NOR DO ANY WOMEN WEAR TWO PIECE SPACE SUITS. SHORING UP, THIS IS A BEACH WHERE THA SHARKS ARE THA ONE'S THAT ARE SELLING ALL THA PROPERTIES. **Legislature** PAGE

(116)

"Taking **your notebook out for a test drive**; I LOVE THA SMELL OF REVOLUTION IN THA MORNING**!**"

(*Tha* IMPORTANCE OF EDUCATION) A moral obligation.

GOVERNMENT ACCOUNTABILITY

Held Ineffective

BU ESS

OLIGARCY! IS THA SPACE STATION READY FOR OCCUPANCY YET?

SIN

Lies, damn lies and ʻ**leadership Failure**ʼ. **reorganization plan**?

➡ WASHINGTON lawmakers

tough Love Letters from Home.

HELLʼ, WOULD BE THA PERFECT PLACE TO LIVE WITHOUT ME, BECAUSE THEN YOU, WOULD HAVE NO-BODYʻLIKE ME, TO QUESTION YOUR JUDGMENT, OR CONSCIOUS."

WASHINGTON SIGNED: 🎼 WE DON'T NEED ANOTHER HERO 🎼

Congratulations, Youʼve Just Been Rejected.

Then and now Your Life Stories REVISITED

Powerful Testimony: PUBLIC — FOR — UM

Specializing in *commonsense* ʻ**Plan for Prosperity**ʼ

(117)

The world according to DR. SUNDAY,
Wit & Wisdom AMAZING VIEWS
News, notes, quips & quotes
`Vintage Journalism REVIEW & TAKEOFF POINT

☞ IF YOU SEE SOMETHING HERE SAY SOMETHING !

☞ JAN.2019 = GOV. SHUTDOWN??? 'RESTING ON THEIR LAURELS AND HARDY' VIA THE SUCCESSFUL 'TARIFF WARS' $$$ THAT BORDER WALL SHOULD HAVE ALREADY BEEN BUILT??? ¨

☞ YOURS TRULY, GROUNDBREAKING NEWS 2002, COMEDY CLUB: DADDY; WHAT'S GROUNDHOG DAY??? 'THAT'S WHEN OSAMA BIN LADEN, CRAWLS OUT OF HIS CAVE; AND IF HE SEE'S HIS SHADOW - THAT MEANS WE'VE GOT '6 MORE WEEKS OF TERRORISM!!!

☞ GREAT JOB PRES. OBAMA! 'ON YOUR WATCH ISIL NEVER HURT ANYONE; BUT IT WAS THE ONE'S THAT CLAIMED TO BE ISIS, THAT PUT A REAL NUMBER ON US...

☞ IN REFERENCE TO THE RUSSIANS HACKING OUR ELECTION WITH 'VOTES? - I DIDN'T KNOW WE HAD THAT MANY PEOPLE LIVING IN MOSCOW IDAHO!!! ¨

☞ I WAS HOPING FOR A HILLARY, ELIZABETH WARREN TICKET; THIS WAY WE'D GET 8 MORE SEASONS, OF WATCHING LAVERN AND SHIRLEY. ☺

☞ 'REALITY CHECK' ON HILLARY'S BOOK!! `MINUS THE #METOO SEX-OFFENDERS, PEDOPHILES, DRUG PUSHERS, BULLIES, RACIST, AND CON-ARTIST, ETC. 'IT TAKES WHAT'S LEFT OF A VILLAGE'. ME!...

☞ ANYMORE NOW, INSTEAD OF SENDING THEIR 'POLITICALLY ASPIRING' KIDS OFF TO COLLEGE TO BECOME POLITICIANS; THEY NOW JUST SEND THEM ALL OFF TO USED CAR SALESMANSHIP SCHOOL... ¨

☞ POLITICALLY SPEAKING, YOURS TRULY, 'IS A NO WOODEN NICKLES TAKING CONSERVATIVE; HEART OF GOLD PROGRESSIVE, LIBERTARIAN...

☞ HELL YEAH! WITHOUT PLANNED PARENTHOOD; THERE'S ALWAYS PLANNED COAT HANGER. SIGNED: HEAVY-DUTY INTO BIRTH CONTROL...

☞ DESPONDENT TAXPAYERS $!$, NOSTRIL-DAMUS PREDICTS: IN THE YEAR 2050, A.K.A. WHEN WE FINALLY EXIT FROM AFGHANISTAN, THE `QURAN COMPATIBLE TALIBAN, WILL JUST WALK RIGHT IN THERE AND TAKE OVER; - OR JUST THE SAME - SHOULD WE LEAVE THERE BY NEXT MONDAY!!!

☞ TO MAKE'UM THINK, IS TO MAKE'UM BLINK! 'IRAN, ALWAYS RE- MEMBER IN USING A NUKE YOU GET 5 MINUTES OF NEW YEAR'S EVE CELEBRATION; THAN IT'S YOUR TURN TO BURN... 3/15

☞ A.K.A. NOSTRIL-DAMUS, PREDICTS THAT THEY'LL BE CLASS-ACTION LAW SUITS WITH MARIJUANA SMOKING AS THERE WERE WITH CIGARETTES!!!

☞ "HOUSTON, I THINK WE HAVE A PROBLEM" 'EVERYONE WANTS TO FIND A NEW PLANET WHERE THEY CAN TAKE ALL THEIR SAME OLD SINS WITH THEM AND START LIFE OVER; WHEN IN FACT WE JUST NEED TO FIX THE ONE WE'RE ALREADY LIVING IN!·...

More evidence 'by pen' AS WE SEE that truı̆ is stranger than fiction

MID·WINTER 1983: PENNILESS AS I STOOD IN THA BLOCK LONG SOUP LINE, THAT WAS TO BE MY ONLY SOURCE OF NUTRITION FOR THA NEXT 4 MONTHS. THA CURIOSITY OF THA OTHER UNFORTUNATE COULD NOT RESIST, BUT ASK ME. "WHATS A CLEAN CUT SILVER SCREEN LOOKING TYPE DUDE LIKE YOU, DOING STANDING IN THA SOUP LINE?" AND I RESPONED TO THEM. "MY HONESTY GOT ME HERE." WHERE BY PROGNOSTICLY, AS I STAND BEFORE THA MIND'S OF THA AMERICAN PEOPLE TO BE YOUR SUIGENERIS PRESIDENT, THEY NEED NOT BE ASKING . . . .

Leadership, Solutions. ACCESSING THA FUTURE

THA PERTINENT PRIORITY'S OF A PROMETHEAN PROMULGATOR, OR PUPPET ON THA PODIUM.

ANNOUNCEMENTS

"I NEVER GREW UP WANTING TO BECOME PRESIDENT, I ONLY GREW UP IN WANTING FOR A BETTER WORLD."

(**Third party**) Independent Lion party presidential candidate.

OVER QUALIFIED TO BECOME PRESIDENT

Lefty Just Wants Things Right.

"NOBODY HAS THA ABILITY TO FOCUS WHEN THEIR DRUGS ARE HOCUS POCUS."

"MEDIA PRODUCTS, 37 YEARS AGO 1983, I SENT A LETTER TO THA REAGAN ADMINISTRATION IN DIRE COMPLAINT ABOUT THA OVER ALL GLAMORIZATION OF DRUGS AND CRIME IN THA MOTION PICTURE INDUSTRY! AND HE NEVER WROTE BACK TO THANK ME.

Mr. President

There's more to us than just taxes.

Where do we go from here?

DEAR PRESIDENT George Bush., March 1989 : SOLVING Peter Pan's performance problems in NEVER-NEVERLAND?

"THA REASON THEY CALL IT DOPE IS THAT, NOBODY INTELLIGENT IS TAKING IT!" (120)

Minimum wage movement
AND The American DREAM !

" Reality Check √ **All In The Family**, I specialize in solutions."

(((DON'T LET THINGS GET UGLY.)))

▼ " **D**ivine inspiration ; INVISIBLE GUIDING."

YOURS TRULY, "BANNED BY THE 'NATIONWIDE MEDIA"
- 2013 -
- AS WAS WRITTEN   *jobs report* JUSTICE PROPOSAL' **covered up.**
AT 'THAT TIME!!!

" **When words need to be said** " PAGE (122)

(((ANSWERS TO: YOURS TRULY, STANDARDIZED MINIMUN WAGE, PLUS BONUSES PROPOSAL.)))

═══════►WORKING AT McDONALD'S, AND MAKING McDONALD DOUGLAS WAGES. ☺

-FEATURING- 'THE "R-E-A-L" SPIN STOPS HERE' 'BY THE MONK AMONG YOU'
CAMPAIGNING FOR - **as is** THE MINIMUM WAGE LAW IS NOTHING MORE THAN A FANCY
NAME FOR SLAVERY. WHEREAS, **INFLATION IS QUALITY OF LIFE'S WORST—
NIGHTMARE,** THUS BEING CAUGHT BETWEEN 'A ROCK AND A HARD PLACE!!!

"PRESENTION (VERSUS) IMMORAL BUSINESS PRACTICES"
IN BRIEF: EXAMPLE - $10. FAST FOOD BURGERS ETC, AND MASSIVE LAYOFFS
OR 'MORAL CONSCIOUSNESS, WOULD BE TO PROVIDE PERIODIC $BONUSES
TO THESE DESERVED WORKERS'... SIGNED: % ARBITRATOR.
"ALL BASED ON AN OVER-ALL QUARTERLY 'PROFIT MARGINAL PERCENTAGE"!
THUS FREE-B UNION WITH GOD (((VERSUS))) OUT OF POCKET $$$ UNIONS.

In my words 'Tha pursuit of happiness is nothing but a — Con—stitution.'

NATIONWIDE truth " THA MINIMUN WAGE LAW,
IS NOTHING MORE THAN A
FANCY NAME FOR SLAVERY."

ALL ONE BIG
SUE CITY
IOWA
AMERICA

IN OTHER WORDS SAFARI AS
I KNOW, IF YOU UNEARTHED THA
FOUNDING FOREFATHERS AND ASKED
THEM IF THEY EVER OWNED ANY SLAVES ?
THEIR RESPONCE WOULD HAVE BEEN! "WERE YOU REFERING TO OUR
EMPLOYMENT OF MINIMUN WAGE WORKERS ?" **reform plan-**
A REVOLUTIONARY PREACHER'S **mind** is a terrible thing to waste. ●

Educational Backround:
YOUR QUESTIONS ANSWERED

I WAS A STRAIGHT A STUDENT,
IN JIM CLASS **! Send in the Clowns.**

RÉSUMÉ FOLLOW-UP:

Licensed to work as

A G.I. BILL PSYCHOLOGY MAJOR; WHEREAS, I STUDIED ABROAD AND SHE TAUGHT
ME EVERYTHING I KNOW! HOW WERE MY GRADES IN SCHOOL? EVERYTIME THEY GAVE
US A BLOOD TEST, I ALWAYS GOT 'A PLUS; — CAN YOU SAY THAT?

RIPE FOR JUDGEMENT
THE REASON I DON'T HAVE OR OWN A GUN IS THAT THEY COST TO MUCH;
I'D PROBABLY HAVE TO GO OUT AND BUY ME A BRAND NEW TV, EVERYWEEK!!!

— MY THESIS WAS IN WORLD GEOGRAPHY;

WHERE I CONVINCED ALL MY CLASSMATES AND TEACHERS;

THAT I HAD BEEN AROUND THE BLOCK A FEW TIMES,

DURING THE TIME WHEN I, WAS A MEMBER OF THE

WI-FI FRATERNITY. — PAPER TRIAL LEAD

TO MY GRADUATING FROM PROFESSIONAL BARTENDING SCHOOL; AND WORKED FOR THE
MOST-PART OF THE NEXT 40 YEARS, INCOGNITO AS A SHRINK. - IN CHICAGO, L.A.
RENO/SPARKS, THUS BECOMING MENTAL HEALTH CARES FINEST; OR BOOK PROOF THERE-
OF IN HOW I BECAME ACCREDITED IN BECOMING YOUR NEW SIGMUND FREUD...

Take Note: Founder of THE POSITIVE Faith Religion;
Heavenly Knowledge uniquely qualified
in a league of his own.

WHEREAS HE **NEVER** QUITS DOING HIS HOMEWORK.

GREAT PHILOSOPHERS
(((PROMOTE DEMOCRACY)))
(New Age Marketing Program)

"DEMOCRACY (FREE SPEACH) IS A MATHEMATICAL
EQUATION, THUS LACK THERE OF COULD
ESCALATE TO A NUCLEAR HOLOCAUST." (123)

Who said that? PAGE (124)

Journalism

It's intellectual prostitution

Try this one on for size.

John Swinton, formerly of the New York Times and called by his peers "the dean of his profession," was asked in 1953 to give a toast before the New York Press Club. He said:

"There is no such thing at this date of the world's history in America as an independent press. . . . There is not one of you who dares to write your honest opinions, and if you did you know beforehand that it would never appear in print. I am paid weekly for keeping my honest opinion out of the paper. . . . (A)ny of you who would be so foolish as to write honest opinions would be out on the street looking for another job. . . . The business of journalism is to destroy truth; to lie outright; to pervert; to vilify; to fawn at the feet of mammon and to sell his country and his race for his daily bread. . . . We are tools and vassals of the rich men behind the scenes. We are the jumping jacks; they pull the strings and we dance. Our talents, our possibilities and our lives are all the property of other men. We are intellectual prostitutes."

And I once thought I wanted to be a reporter.

Quote **Clovis Bull,** *Reno*

controversy isn't going away.

choose revolution or status quo
The end of silence

TV, JOURNALIST ETC'

WE'RE NOT GONNA TAKE IT ANYMORE BEGINS HERE.

If not now, when? There's more to us than just taxes.

Positive news 1999

WEIGHT FOR ME:

YOURS TRULY "1st, TO PROMOTE THIS FORMULAIC COMMONSENSE DIET.")))

LIVING LIFE IN THA FAST FOOD LANE?

`INTRODUCING THA Dr. SUNDAY, Diet!´

`YOU GET TO EAT EVERYDAY LIKE itS THANKSGIVING., SO DEPENDING ON YOUR OVER-ALL CALORIE INTAKE, ONE MAY ONLY HAVE TO DO UP TO 3 TO 4 HRS, of HIT THA GROUND RUNNING, DAILY PHYSICAL FITNESS ACTIVITY, TO COMPENSATE!

AUTHOR'S NOTE: IN ALL REALITY THA BEST DIET IS REALLY THA SWISS CHEESE DIET!
— YOU JUST EAT THA HOLES...

Interview factory original

When show Business Met DR. Sunday

Question DO I BELIEVE IN MIRACLES? STORY ANSWERS TO; — WELL SORT OF!!!

"I COULD NEVER REMEMBER HIS NAME

BUT, — THERE ONCE WAS THIS BALD HEADED GUY I KNEW, WITH A SEVERE CASE OF CRIPPLING ARTHRITIS; — AND HE ASKED ME TO PRAY FOR HIM. (SO I DID!) AND

HE ENDED UP WITH A FULL HEAD OF HAIR"...

"I WANT TO LIVE IN A WORLD WHERE VANITY BECOMES THA WORSE SIN ON THA PLANET., BECAUSE THEN ALL PIGGIES, WILL HAVE BECOME NON-EXISTENT."

(125)

Explaining Everything

How to Interpret That Heavenly Knowledge

STEP RIGHT UP

I'M JUST. HOME COOKING A GOOD EGG'O WITH THA RIGHT TYPE OF EGO, AND PHEASANT PERSONALITY THAT WOULDN'T FRY, SCRAMBLE, OR HARD BOIL YOU. THA EGGCEPTIONAL KIND OF EGG SAMPLE OVER EASY YOKER, YOU SHELL EGGSPECT TO CRACK UP WITH OSTRICH OF THA IMAGINATION, JUST BY EGGING ME ON. 'SO WITHOUT GETTING EGGCITED! OM'ELET YOU DECIDE TO BENEDICT CHICKEN CATCH A TORREZ, BY EGG SPELLING CHICKEN ALA KING, AND QUICHE THA WHOLE HUMPTY DUMPTY SYSTEM GOOD BY., BECAUSE I'M NOT A FREUD of UGLY DUCKING ANY ISSUE, I'M EGGSTREMELY CAPON ABLE OF EGGSPERTLY EGGSPRESSING MYSELF - BEAKING IN TONGUES, LIKE A TRUE EGGSTROVERT.

NERD Power SIGNED

THA FOWL MOUTH EGGHEAD, OR GEEK MYTHOLOGY MAJOR YOU CAN INCUBATE ON, WILL TRY NOT TO RUFFLE ANYONE'S FEATHERS. Page (126) JUST HATCHED

Kinder? Gentler? STOP THA WORLD—

I WANT TO GET ON! **LEARN ABOUT** FREEDOM

of PROMOTIONAL RELIGIOUS & POLITICAL EXPRESSION,

Honoring Divine Inspiration?  The POSITIVE SPIRIT long reach:

Bringing To Life Criticism ignored by tha

media! SIGNED YOURS TRULY, CONGRESSIONAL

MEDAL of HONOR WINNER IN THA WAR OF THA

COLD SHOULDER. ——— I'M STILL ———

—AWAITING YOUR RETURN CALL?

Imagemakers "stop this cover-up!"

YOURS TRULY, IN BRIEF ON
BECOMING CAR-CZAR
SALESMAN OF THA YEAR?
—OR HOW I BECOME SAVIOR
OF THA AUTO INDUSTRY!
I'D RE-MAKE, RETROFIT,
BRING BACK 'ALL THA
MUSCLE CARS ETC, OF
THA 50's & 60's,..
PRICED WITHIN REASON, THEY'D
ALL SELL LIKE HOT-CAKES...

JAMAICA MY DAY.

**Call me today
I specialize
in solutions.**

Atrocities of Democracy. Calendar of Events

STORY-LINE 1980,. *featuring* CONSECUTIVE YEARS!

THA BATTLE AGAINST TIME. PAGE (127)

The Book That Reveals
The Whole Shocking Truth

VOTER ALERT !

on representation **Who Counts, & Who Don't** ?

WHERE WE ARE NOW

The Secret History **of** Plutocracy

(Government by the Rich.)

C H R O N I C L E S

HIGHLIGHT
The Second Coming
of Democracy
FACTORY TO YOU !

WE'VE COME A LONG WAY
SINCE CHARIOT RACING.

HAD ENOUGH
FEATURES

The Man Who Saved Democracy

The Untold Stories

The Muzzling OF the Press

A Voice Silenced !

Get ready for truth support

Inquiring Minds Want to Know: PAGE (128)

READING REVOLUTION
"Storytelling on a grand scale"
Nobody beats him in blame game !
Based on Notebooks
Powerful Testimony
CHARTING A NEW COURSE
redefining our politics.
YOU ARE HERE
Objectivity
The Secret Societies
LAST DAYS OF
Downsizing Democracy
Featured Prize
THE HUMPTY DUMPTY
PLUTOCRATIC
SYSTEM

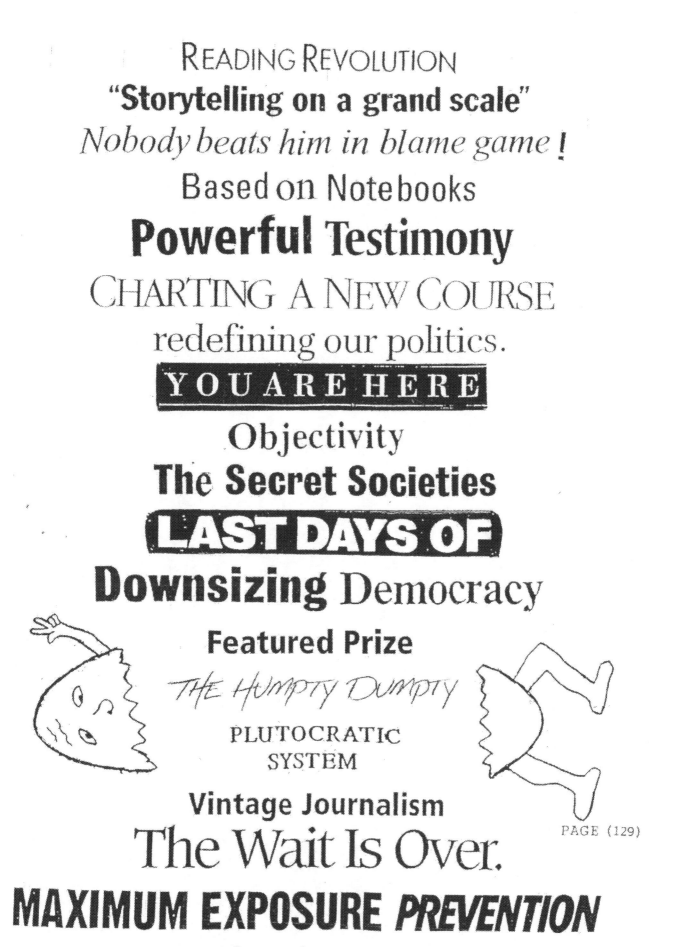

Vintage Journalism
The Wait Is Over.

MAXIMUM EXPOSURE *PREVENTION*
That was then...

A PROMISE FULFILLED

DELIVERS.

redefining our politics.

YOU ARE HERE

Vintage Journalism

The Wait Is Over.

Reality Check Be Prepared To Be Impressed.

"read this book!"

AND

God Let Us Find Him

Blessed to live in Reno

HISTORY WILL BE STAGED.

STEP BY STEP, *A Whole New*

Constitutional freedom *Phenomenon.*

"A Hidden World Discovery Kit

For THIS Voice of the Voiceless, *is*

The `Real Day The Earth Stood Still ...

Author Biography A biography of tha writer of that book. So please let us know a little about you. where you live, and other pertinent highlights about your interests:

1988
RENO NEVADA: THA TRIALS AND TRIBULATIONS OF GOING ABOUT AND BEING AN UNRECOGNIZABLE SUPERSTAR, LIVING IN A ONE HORSE TOWN, AND LOVING EVERY MINUTE OF IT.

formula for "**Peace On Earth**" *thus*
a *Marketing lesson from God is a*
'ONE WORLD RELIGION'.
religion at the ballot box brings you
A 'POSITIVE ENTITY OF BILLIONS

everyone succeeds
FROM **MULTIPLE SOLUTIONS.**

WORLD FUTURE SOCIETY

INFORMATION SUPERHIGHWAY
OFFICIAL NOTIFICATION

NEW-AGE
Concepts For Positive Living

1
GOD
The Positive Spirit
WITHOUT
Gender

((LOGO))

'Plan for Prosperity'

WITH THE CHURCH
'SERMON CITY'
Business
You Can Trust •

♫ THE FINAL COUNT DOWN ♫

BORN ON A BIO ♫ *"It's The End Of World As We Know It"*

The world according to DR. SUNDAY,

'MAKE A DIFFERENCE ENDER'S GAME'

<u>'POLICE</u> STATE' THAT THE DOCTOR WILL SEE YOU NOW...

'political religious revolution'

Guidelines: "PEACEFUL 'EVOLUTION, REVOLUTION,
IS THE SOLUTION TO BE FREE OF MENTAL POLUTION."

"PATRIOTISM IS THE BACKBONE OF OUR COUNTRY!
YOURS TRULY, BEST RESTORER OF!"

THE SEARCH FOR SIGNS OF INTELLIGENT LIFE IN THE UNIVERSE

YOUR GUIDE TO *The Real Day The Earth Stood Still* ((COUNTDOWN))

OUTTA THIS WORLD AND ON WITH THE NEXT..

'WILL OF GOD TESTIMONY' TAKES 'YOU TO ME LEADER!

'ALIEN LINGUAL ▬ 'DIT JUNEAU RAT NOW, DAT OLIVE IN WE KNOW!

♫ MEET THE NEW BOSS-'<u>NOT</u>'THE SAME AS THE OLD BOSS.

rhetoric of revolution **I specialize in solutions!**

"FOR WHAT STARTED WITH 'RELIGION, CAN ONLY BE 'RECTIFIED BY RELIGION!!!"

You are now officially out of excuses, "THY WILL BE DONE".

BETTER LIVING THROUGH DISCOVERY

FINALLY... <u>LIFE</u> INSURANCE YOU CAN AFFORD

'WAKE UP AND SMELL THE C-O-P-Y' OF A Democracy **Prison** Original.

IN BRIEF: HOW TO SAY SOMETHING IN SO MANY WORDS.

<u>EXPERIENCE</u> <u>HAVING A BEAUTIFUL MIND.</u>

- IN TEACHING PEOPLE HOW TO BECOME 'FRANK WITHOUT THE BUN!

DR. SUNDAY Discovery Kit PAGE (132)

((ANSWERS TO MYSTERIOUS END OF AN AGE PROPHECY FULFILLED))

OR 'HELL, WHAT'S A NICE GUY LIKE ME DOING IN A PLACE LIKE THIS?

iF

RENO'S BEST TOURIST ATTRACTION!

BOOK REVIEW

"TESTIMONIALS:

PAGE (133)

My BOOK SHOULD SELL!

or DEVIL FORBID, "IF ENOUGH PEOPLE CRY WOLF."

written OPINION COMMENTARY

15-CENTURIES of UP in coming FAME,

OUTTA THIS WORLD AND ON WITH THA NEXT!!!

FOR THA LOVE of ~~MONEY~~ GOD, EVERYTHING'S going TO BE ALRIGHT.

And They Lived Happily Ever After"...

BETTER LIVING THROUGH DISCOVERY

freedom calls for competition.'

Critics Investigation shows

they're running out of excuses

GREAT VIBES!

" *The Gospel according to* **If you Build This** "

THEY'LL BE A RECTITUDE'L OF THA MOODLE BY WAY OF MYSTICAL ENLIGHTENMENT...

VALIDATION TIME FOR

'REVOLUTIONARY PREACHER'

How would religion respond to discovery of aliens?

THE SEARCH FOR SIGNS OF INTELLIGENT LIFE IN THE UNIVERSE!

'The world is watching'

EVIDENCE

TO HAVING A PLANETARY ORIGIN,

THUS BEING SOLAR SYSTEM IMPRINT DESIGNED!!!

Tell It Like It Is

"WE'RE ALL VISITORS OF THIS PLANET, PLAN IT. — *Me* 1980"

TAKING STOCK of statements put on paper "I AM -

THE MOST INTERESTING MAN IN THE World."

Looking to pound home a message "YOU NEED ME".

Lessons learned from Positive INFLUENCE!

The capitalist who believes we can all capitalize together...

'THE PROPHET THAT BELIEVES IN PROFIT SHARING'...

EXPERIENCE HAVING A BEAUTIFUL MIND.

THIS HERE BEING A HOW TO GUIDE!

"STOP THE WORLD 'I, WANT TO GET ON!"

FAITH FORUM QUESTION ON:

MOST INSPIRING RELIGIOUS FIGURE? ANSWERS TO:

" ALL THIS HASN'T BEEN GIVEN TO ME FOR NOTHING."

Larry looks back on his legacy

A Celebration of Faith

If not this, what? If not now, when?

"'This Is My Life' Years haven't been kind. words surely can change meanings.

F-O-R REPLACEMENT C-H-R-I-S-T S-A-K-E ,
'M-A-K-E 'MY' L-I-F-E'

DOCTOR'S BOOK OF NEW World REMEDIES

A UNIQUE SOURCE of SUPERIOR WISDOM

(ON Controversial Issues)

MAXIMUM EXPOSURE PREVENTION!

Say It Ain't So. Tell It Like It Is...

"BOOK'S PARALLEL EPILOGUE: AND DEAR GOD, NO NEED TO
FORGIVE ANYONE NOW = FOR THEY KNOW NOW WHAT THEY DO!".

"AS I STATED IN LIFE, I'LL STATE BY WAY OF MY PASSING;
DON'T PRAY TO 'ME ---'PRAY TO GOD"...

Tha big picture In Testimony Whereof

('WHEN YOUR THIS COMPLETE, THEY'LL BE NO NEED FOR MY 2ND COMING'.)

Live from tha cemetery Set my news free.

Once Upon A Time,

With ALL MY, OVER-ALL PROPOSED BENEFICIAL CONTRIBUTIONS
TOWARDS THA BETTERMENT OF MANKIND; OF ALL THA FLESH AND
BLOOD PEOPLE, THAT HAVE 'EVER SET FOOT ON THIS PLANET!

---'I WOULD HAVE CHOSE TO BE ME!"

THIS BOOK'S PROGRAM DEVELOPMENT WAS ALL DONE WITHOUT THA
USE OF ANY PERFORMANCE ENHANCING (H.G.H.) STEROIDS, OR OPIOIDS,

ETC. now, How do you like me ?

Teaching THE Good Book as a Textbook
WITHOUT THE SPEED BUMPS
READING REVOLUTION
"Storytelling on a grand scale"

Dr. Sunday is the founder of The Positive Faith Religion; a Lobbyist for God who lays claim to a Ministry of Higher Education. "Always was and always will be God, is The HOLY SPIRIT 'positive spirit = without gender." "All God's children!"

"The world according to The MESSIAH!"
Wit & Wisdom AMAZING VIEWS
News, notes, quips & quotes
Observations, confessions and revelations

INNERSOUL SUPPORT SYSTEM 'Presenting God's inspired word:

How to Interpret That Heavenly Knowledge
What Saith The Scriptures

'BOOK FORTIFIED, AS ONE'S LIFE IMPROVES'
DON'T PRAISE ME; PRAISE GOD...

DON'T Thank (((Me,))) Thank GOD.

defining mission a must read
of presentation, "**Let freedom truly reign!**

NEWS OF RECORD on **NATIONWIDE Gunman** GONE WILD, <u>ETC</u>!.

Someone must stand up to our government

"THEY CAN'T PROTECT US!. ONLY THRU "THIS HERE SAME **book**
UNIFIED MORAL REVOLUTION" WILL NORMALCY EVER PREVAIL"...
'WAKE UP AND SMELL THE C-O-P-Y'

WHO AM I? I'M THE DEVIL'S WORST 'BEAN SPILLING ON' NIGHTMARE!

"In this man's religion there's God in man, but there's no such thing as a man that's GOD."

<u>ENTER CLASSROOM SAVIOR OF THE WORLD</u>

RIGHT FROM WRONG, GOOD FROM EVIL, ON RELIGION? GIVE ME 'ALL YOUR FLUNKIES! YOU DON'T NEED
A WAFER COMMUNION TO BE IN SYNC WITH THIS CRACKER. A MAN HAS GOT TO KNOW 'HIS SAME PAGE
RELIGIOUS LIMITATIONS, OR THE WHOLE WORLD JUST ALL BECOMES A 'GO TO HELL SOCIETY! - AS
LIKE IN AL-QAIDA'S 'DOGMA, IT'S ALL JUST FOAMING AT THE MOUTH...

TO ALL MY RELIGIOUS COMPETITORS "WHEN YOUR DOGMA QUITS BARKING

FREEDOM OF CHOICE' IS FOR YOU TO PREACH 'MY GOSPEL AND KEEP ALL YOUR
$$$ PARISHIONERS, OR SUFFER THE CONSEQUENCES OF HEAVY DUTY COMPETITION.

Imagemakers "stop this cover-up!"

"This is what `I was put on earth to do".

"TILL DEATH DO US PART; CHRISTIANITY OR 'ETC, WILL <u>NEVER</u> CONVERT ISLAM, AND VICE VERSA"

'RIGHTEOUSLY COMBATING MADNESS'

"THIS HERE BEING A 'PEACE ON EARTH, 'ONE WORLD RELIGION' PROPOSAL"

* *And best Quote of the Campaign award goes to*

The <u>real deal</u>, is now **Stand and deliver.**

WHO AM I? "I AM THE "GLOBAL" 'WOMENS RIGHTS' ABRAHAM LINCOLN,

Don't deprive me of my right to be

YOU CAN'T FAKE PAGE (137)

F-O-R REPLACEMENT C-H-R-I-S-T S-A-K-E , YOURS TRULY "THE
* MAHDI' MESSIAH, CHOSEN ONE" **'THY WILL BE DONE'**

'WITH PUBLISHERS CLEARING HOUSE, 'TWO FOR ONE' CLOSE-OUT SALE!!!

OUTTA THIS WORLD AND ON WITH THE NEXT **READY OR NOT, DAY HAS ARRIVED.**

This is the end.

TODAY I MUST CONFESS

"WE COULD BE IN STORE FOR SOMEWHAT OF A MILD WINTER!" :)

*Without **TRUTH** our world could not go on.*

A way into the system
aims to 'revitalize' society

miracle on **138** th / page ARE WE THERE YET?

Your Audience Needs to Know!

Happenings Around Town

People in Support.
Tha Beginning:

SIGNED official :

A B C'er of ROBOT SCHOOL.

ARE PEOPLE TREATING YOU LIKE AN ALIEN?

"IN THIS MAN'S RELIGION THERE'S GOD IN MAN,
BUT THERE'S NO SUCH <u>THING</u> AS A MAN THAT'S GOD!"

THE GOSPEL ACCORDING TO A CONCLUSION!

YOUR GUIDE TO *The Real Day The Earth Stood Still* (((COUNTDOWN)))
*'Warning' to Russian, or Martian and celebrate a structured man is a
'dooms day scenario.' Whereas there's only one God, reeling in the diving light line,
out of sight 'positive'* SPIRIT *in the sky...*

TIME SENSITIVE

- WITH ALL THE ON GOING EFFECTS OF 'CLIMATE CHANGE' HAPPENING;
  IT'S NOW LIKE TELLING YOUR CHILDREN; - <u>SORRY KID'S</u>; WE GAVE
  AWAY ALL OF YOUR ENVIRONMENTAL INHERITANCE TO THE DEVIL...

  ♫ FROM JUST A HUNDRED POUNDS OF CLAY;
     - TO ALL WE ARE IS DUST IN THE WIND. ♫

  I NOAH' AN AWFUL LOT ABOUT LOVE BOAT SURVIVAL.
     - IN OTHER WORDS; IF WE DON'T CRITIQUE; WE'LL
  CURTAIL; AND EVERYONE WILL BE SWALLOWED BY THE WHALE... ☹

                                    —— SUNDAY

Printed in the United States
By Bookmasters